Healing Infidelity

How to Build a Vibrant Marriage After an Affair

Rick Copple
Lenita Copple

Published by Ethereal Press

ISBN: 978-0615821207
1st Edition

Disclaimers: Rick and Lenita Copple do not claim to be certified therapists. Nothing in this book should be received as advice for a specific person or situation.

Other than the authors, all names have been changed to protect the innocent and the guilty. General statements should not be interpreted as having any one particular individual in mind.

Table of Contents

Preface

We wrote this book to answer one primary question: what does a healthy rebuilding after infidelity that results in a vibrant marriage look like? In the following pages you will read our story and what we did that resulted in a marriage richer than it was before the affairs.

Before we dig into that, we need to explain how this book was written, lest there be any confusion. The primary writer of this book is me, Rick Copple, husband of Lenita Copple. Because I have written the book, I've told our story primarily from my point of view rather than pretending to write from her point of view as well. We considered her writing parts of this, and that route would have had its benefits, but our problem is she works so much that she struggled merely to edit the book. If she wrote much of the content, the book would never have been written.

For that reason, and that I have writing experience, we both opted for me to write it, and she would go back through it to correct me when my memory failed, offer different ways of wording, or include information I had unintentionally left out. Due to that, our story is written from my point of view, though I fill in details I didn't know at the time that I later learned from her.

So why is she listed as a co-author? Aside from stamping her own viewpoint into my words through edits, because she and I have, through this experience, written the content of this story together. I'm merely reporting in an organized fashion what happened. She wrote this story with her decisions. First in succumbing to an affair and, after that, by her commitment to rebuild. Additionally, she wrote the outline for the chapter "Healing Steps for the Unfaithful Spouse."

With that bit of information clarified, let us begin the task of showing and instructing on how a marriage that has gone through the horrors of infidelity can come out the other end, vibrant, fulfilled, and thriving.

Introduction

"It will never happen to me." Ever think that? Okay, I knew my wife cheating on me wasn't out of the realm of possibility, but I seriously thought the chance it would happen was a million to one. I thought we loved each other enough, were committed Christians enough, that such an event would never touch our marital doorstep. After 29 years of marriage, I thought I knew her inside and out. Indeed, anyone who knew us would be just as surprised.

After we were engaged, but before the marriage, we made a pact that we would never joke about divorce, and that we would always be honest with each other. We kept that pack for over 28 years. I had no reason to believe that would ever change. Sure, we each had our little secrets, but nothing like infidelity.

This book contains the story of how my wife fell into temptation and had an affair, and how we rebuilt our relationship and marriage from those ashes. It was difficult and painful for both of us. But the resulting relationship with her is richer and deeper than ever before.

No, I'm not promoting infidelity as the new marriage enrichment tool. It destroys more marriages than it helps. Our example is, unfortunately, in the minority. We offer this story and the following articles in the hope that it will illustrate how a marriage can go through the roughest test of love and come out on top. We offer it to show one example of what a positive rebuilding looks like.

One note before we proceed. It is easy to look at what my wife did and say, "Bad woman! I would never do that!" And you may be right. But more often than not, that attitude leaves one vulnerable to the lure of temptation. It often causes people to ignore boundaries. My wife, Lenita, thought just that. She never imagined she would cheat on me. But by the time she realized she was, it was too late. She already had.

One might think, especially at the beginning of this story, that I think little of my wife. That I should hate her, or that this story is told to shame her. Nothing could be further from the truth. Indeed, how she handled the recovery and rebuilding puts me to shame. Her repentance and work on herself proved her love for me. I loved her through the whole painful process and will continue to do so.

She agreed to go public with this story, despite her reservations of how some people might respond to her, because she knows it can help people who have or are going through this situation. This has been proven by our interaction anonymously on a support group. Her willingness to do this is just one example of why I admire her so much. She is willing to risk her own reputation if it will help others going through infidelity. It is this attitude that she has taken through the whole rebuilding process and continues to this day. I could not be more proud of her.

Following is the story of what has become the most painful time of our lives as well as the most life-changing journey we've ever undertaken. May you find aid, strength, inspiration, and renewed hope in the pages that follow.

Part 1 - Our Story

The Unbelievable

Wednesday morning, around 2:00 am, May 11, 2011. I sat in front of the computer screen in our living room early that morning, reading a key log of my wife's activity on the computer. I expected to find evidence of online sex chatting, maybe shared photos, or at worst, some phone sex.

I had braced myself to see that, so when it became obvious in reading the log that she had committed those deeds, it didn't shock me. I knew I would need to talk with her about her secret life and have her end the online activity, but I didn't see it as any great revelation. I'd already suspected it. But I was naive about affairs. I didn't know there were such things as emotional affairs, without the sex. I didn't view it on the same level.

But I wasn't prepared for her confession to her online sex chatting buddy. I wasn't prepared to discover that she'd been having sex with a local man for up to six weeks. Actually, I thought initially it might be two different guys by the way she talked, but it was only one guy. I wasn't prepared to discover that several months ago, she'd committed a physical, non-intercourse sex act with another man.

After reading that revelation, I had to walk away. I sat in our living room chair and repeated to myself several times, "No, no, no, no!" What she had confessed went against everything I knew about her and our relationship. I couldn't believe what I had read. Yet, there it was, in black and white, in her own words.

Was she just playing a game with that guy? He was discussing his desire to commit adultery on his wife because she didn't want to have sex with him at all. He'd grown frustrated. His confession of his desire had triggered her into confessing, for the first time to anyone, about her own affair.

But her descriptions were too specific and matched too closely to what I knew to be a made-up story. She even compared me and the other man in how we performed in bed. Though I hoped beyond hope that what I read wasn't true, I knew the chance of it being a story that she had created out of thin air was slim.

The shock was more than just her cheating on me, but why? We loved one another. I'd seen no indications that she was unhappy. The last several months, our sex life had even been on fire. Little did I know that her affairs had generated that sexual energy.

But that wasn't the whole of it. Our 29th anniversary was only four days away, on May 15th. Our marriage wasn't perfect, but from all indications, she loved me very much and I loved her. As I will detail later, we weren't meeting each other's romantic needs as we should have been. We'd been through some difficult times in the past, but came through them all right.

We have three children. The youngest ended his junior year in high school by that point. Of the older two, one had moved out some years ago and the other stayed because of learning disabilities and still needing to learn to live independently. Lenita and I had a long history together, going through some rough times. I loved her and, for all I knew up to that point, she loved me.

But that wasn't the totality of why that revelation shocked me. The truth is that to that date, I'd never been with another woman and she'd never been with another man. I treasured that relationship because to me it was the ultimate intimacy. No man other than me had been intimate with her, and no woman other than her had been sexual with me. Throughout our lives, the only two people allowed into that intimate room was her and I.

I thought we shared the same values. I thought we both believed the fact that we'd reserved ourselves exclusively for each other was of great worth. I thought that was more important to her than discovering how other men felt and worked. But that night, the truth that had held up for 28½ years had been broken. Our wedding vows had been violated. Another man had joined with my wife, and it was no longer just me and her in that intimate room.

This was the major loss I experienced that night. I discovered my wife had taken something valuable from me and destroyed it. I realized she, for the first time in our marriage, led a secret life and deceived me about it. I lost my trust in her. I lost my intimacy with her. I lost my sense of her support for me and our life together.

At that point, I had no idea what she thought about our relationship. If she even still loved me or not. Had I done something that caused her to do this? Was she going to leave me once I confronted her about it? I had no clue. I didn't have any indication anything was wrong. But obviously something had gone horribly wrong.

The worse fear that sank into my brain in the early morning hours was that her spiritual condition must be in the pits. She'd sinned a big sin, and her soul was in jeopardy. For the first time in our married life, I realized the chance of me being in heaven but her not making it became real. In short, I had lost her. I had no clue if I would be able to get her back again or not.

I can honestly say that as of that morning, I'd never experienced a greater shock in my life. But for me, that was the beginning of my journey through infidelity. I didn't ask to be taken on this journey. I was signed up for it without my consent. But I was on it, and it was either work to save her, or let her go. I didn't know which route I would end up taking because I didn't know where she stood. I hoped this could be fixed.

So the following chapters reveal my story. What we went through. How we came out the other end. Yes, it has been extremely painful for both of us. We have learned a lot through the process that we hope, as we share with you, may help others who are traveling this dark journey.

Not everything we went through will apply to everyone. Some things others have gone through that we have not. But through struggling in our own journey and reading about countless others journeys in this situation, we think we can offer hope for a better outcome. While there are many differences between what we've gone through and what others have, there are some common principles that can be gleaned from our situation and applied to many others.

I also want to make it clear that I am not a therapist. I've not studied marriage counseling or the like. I have been a pastor and gone through that training. But I don't want anyone to take what I say as coming from a case worker who has counseled many couples over the years and am distilling that wisdom into this book.

No, I'm just a man who has been cheated on, and my wife is a woman who allowed herself to fall into one of the worse sins possible. But there are some things you can't learn through books, but only by the experience of hard knocks. Now that I've had the chance to discuss these issues with others going through adultery in various stages, degrees, and some in a lot worse situations, I believe that I can offer help to those going through infidelity. To let you know you are not alone. To offer hope to the hurt spouse and the unfaithful spouse that there is life beyond infidelity for both, together, if both parties are willing to invest in each other.

The first part is our story. In parts 2 through 4, I'll offer topical articles distilling what we've learned through this experience. But first, we need to go back a few years before May 11, 2011. We need to go back to our dating and marriage.

Housekeeping

Before we get underway, there are a few topics we need to address to avoid misunderstandings. The first is why are we sharing this story? Some may feel voyeuristic reading about these events. I'm certainly aware of that aspect, that we're opening up a private part of our lives to the public. It isn't something we do lightly. Especially for my wife's sake. But we have both agreed to do this for one primary reason: in the hopes that it will help other couples going through this horrible experience to have the best chance of rebuilding to a vibrant marriage. We aren't telling you our story simply so you can say, "Oh, how horrible! At least it turned out good for you." Nor are we looking for sympathy.

Rather, the first reason is to give you our credentials: we've gone through it and come out in better shape than most. Second, to inspire those who are going through this that it can be done. Third, to give you a picture of what a successful rebuilding looks like and to lay out the underlying principles through our story of what went wrong and what went right through the process.

Terms

We also need to define some terms. On the support forum at *Daily Strength* that we've been a part of since I discovered my wife's affairs, the person who was cheated on is labeled "the betrayed spouse," and the one who cheated, "the cheating spouse." Though both parties freely use those terms, I felt I needed less emotionally charged terms. I've seen others use different terminology like "wayward spouse." I've landed on the following terms.

The one who has been cheated on I'm calling the **hurt spouse**. The one who cheated, the **unfaithful spouse**, and the person(s) who helped the unfaithful spouse cheat, the **affair partner(s)**.

I've seen many books use "partner" instead of "spouse" for the hurt and unfaithful spouse. I understand why they prefer that term, since in our society there is often sex before marriage as well as relationships not considered traditional marriage who may not think of their partner as a spouse.

While I acknowledge that reality, it is also the case that marriage is a multifaceted reality, to which I'll devote a chapter later in this book. But here it is enough to know that sexual intercourse, in my understanding, is not only intended for a couple within a marriage, but consummates and finalizes the marital bond even when outside of a legal and emotional commitment to do so.

Because of that bond, sexual intercourse and/or emotional intimacy with someone other than one's spouse is always a violation of a marital bond. So I would suggest that even if one has not signed the legal papers and gone through the ceremony, if you are emotionally, socially, and physically bonded with each other, you are married for the purposes of this book. All you are lacking is the legal bond. If you don't think of yourself or your "significant other" as a spouse, just mentally substitute the word you would use.

In general, the words **infidelity**, **affair**, and **cheating** can all be understood as referring to the same thing: when a spouse invests more emotional and/or physical energy with a person other than his spouse. These are broad terms that encompass everything from talking with someone more than you do with your own spouse, to a one night stand, to a full "falling in love" sexual affair that lasts months or years.

An **emotional affair** is the non-physical side of an affair. An emotional affair is when a spouse invests more emotional energy in someone other than his spouse. Usually this refers to an emotional bond of love developing between a couple—when there is a driving desire in a person to spend time frequently with someone who is not one's spouse due to a "chemistry" between them. The more intimate the discussion, the more clearly this affair exists.

A **physical affair** is exactly what it sounds like: when a spouse gives physical sexual attention to someone other than his spouse. However, this can extend to sexual conversations. While not physical, it is participating in sexual play with another individual whom one is not married to.

In most affairs, there will be a combination of the above two. But it is possible to only have an emotional affair (flirting, intimate conversations, becoming infatuated with someone) or a physical affair (one-night-stands, prostitute, a sex-only relationship). All of it is a form of cheating. I've seen marriages ended over one spouse saying

"I love you" to another person, despite that "nothing happened" physically. Many women consider an emotional affair worse than the physical and don't separate the two so easily.

Adultery, on the other hand, is a narrow subset of the above terms. It involves the act of or strong desire for sexual intercourse with someone other than your spouse. Committing adultery is a form of infidelity, but one can be unfaithful to one's spouse without ever having committed adultery. A fact too many people don't know, including myself before going through this. Adultery is discussed more fully in a chapter later in this book.

Also, to avoid awkward constructions, I'll be using English's generic "he" pronoun to reference both genders when speaking of a whole group. It is only to be interpreted as masculine when referencing particular individuals. Otherwise, it will refer to both sexes.

Disclosures

I need to make clear up front that I am not a trained therapist, marriage counselor, nor have I counseled a whole list of couples going through affairs. My wife and I have been there, done that. We have discussed many of these issues with others going through infidelity. We have read several books on the subject and put into practice their recommendations. What we've learned, we give to you. But by all means, don't make this your one and only stop. As we go along, we'll recommend books that have helped us and many others. But what we offer here isn't a substitute for a therapist or counselor to address your specific situation.

I also want to disclose that I am a Christian and approach this topic from that worldview. Before you close this book and throw it in the trash can, should you be so inclined, allow me to add the following. I'm not going to stuff this book full of Bible quotes and trite Christian platitudes. I'm not out to convert anyone through this book. If it does, it will be because God uses it that way, not because I try to hammer you over the head with Christianity.

No, this is a story that is universal. It transcends religions and races and cultures. Hundreds of years before Christ, God gave Moses the Ten Commandments, one of which was "Thou shalt not commit adultery." This experience has been with us for many, many, many years. Millions of people through history have dealt with adultery and infidelity in every culture and country of this world.

But I am a Christian and approach it unapologetically from that frame of reference. I've obtained a Bachelor of Arts degree in religion, been in seminary, and have pastored two churches. But I believe the principles I'll be presenting in these pages will be applicable across religious and cultural boundaries.

So whether you are Christian or not, don't be afraid to continue on and learn what you can. If you don't agree with something, certainly there is nothing I can do to convince you to agree with me. But I'll do my best to talk common sense that most can agree with and use. All I ask is that you be open and evaluate what I have to say. Then decide for yourself.

I also need to warn the reader, that due to the subject at hand, I will be discussing issues concerning sex in a frank manner. For those that actually know me, be aware that I will be relating some information about our personal sexual life. No graphic or descriptive images, but some people might say, "To much information!" However, to fully discuss this subject requires addressing sexual topics on occasion. Be assured I will do my best to be clear yet discrete. But if discussions of this topic offend you, or you know me and don't want to know how frequently we've had or have sex, then you might want to bow out. At least if you read on, you will have been warned. Nothing titillating, but it is mentioned plainly.

The last issue I wanted to deal with is the difference between marital problems and the "reasons" or "causes" of cheating. All marriages experience difficulties, problems, and rough roads. As I stated in the first chapter, we'd had our share of those. Some of which we'll discuss. But no marriage is immune from times of not feeling as in love or as attracted to one another. This is common to all marriages.

But when a spouse has an affair, it may be based on the reality that such problems make the affair more tempting and compelling than it might have been otherwise. However, the choice to have an affair, either by a conscious decision or by refusal to stop it, is not caused by those problems, but is an inappropriate response to either those problems and/or personal issues of those involved.

So in laying out the problems we have had in our marriage, I am in no manner saying that she is justified in committing adultery, nor am I taking the blame for her decision to do so. I do accept the blame for our marriage not being as rich and good as it could have been. I do accept the blame for making her more vulnerable to temptation. But in the end, it was her decision to respond to a feeling of distance from me by seeking it out in another man. Do not mistake the following chapters as me excusing her behavior, justifying it, or saying that I was to blame for the affairs. She, along with her affair partners take 100% of the blame for that sin.

To blame the hurt spouse for the cheating is the equivalent of the following analogy. You discover your house is on fire. You have two buckets, one containing water and the other gasoline. Does it help the house to throw that bucket of gasoline onto the fire? Of course not, even if it is more exciting to do so. In the same way, choosing an affair as the route to deal with marital problems does not solve them, but makes them far worse.

With those issues out of the way, let's take a tour of my marriage leading up to the last few years.

In the Beginning

We started dating in the summer of 1980. It had been a wild school year previous to that. My first year of college had me fall in love with a woman, get little sleep while racking up a good grade point average, only to have her dump me after coming back from Christmas break. That created a chaotic second semester, which I struggled through the first breakup in my life with an official girlfriend, rebounded a bit, but never really getting my feet back under me.

Long story short, I went to a teen after-glow one Sunday night that following summer. At the party was my wife to be. Up to that point, we'd hung out a good bit here and there, but I had mainly thought of her as this annoying teen. She was attention deprived and annoyed people trying too hard to be liked. But that evening, something changed in my view of her, and I thought to myself, "She's kind of fun to be around."

So after the party, I drove her home, but we ended up going to get a coke together, and then we sat on a lake pier for several hours talking with each other. When I finally dropped her off in the wee hours of the morning, I kissed her goodnight.

I didn't want to commit to anything. I was still recovering from what had happened with the previous girl, and I didn't want to make any promises. But as it turned out, we continued seeing each other and, a few months later, I proposed to her. To be different, I did so while standing on my head. She said yes, and after a year and a half engagement, we were married on May 15, 1982.

We were both very much in love with each other. Being Christians, we had pledged to remain faithful. We promised never to joke about divorce. We were committed to making our marriage work where both our parents had failed. We both came from divorced families due to infidelity and knew firsthand the damage it had caused. We wanted better for ourselves and our future kids.

After that wedding ceremony, we had our whole lives before us, ready to enjoy the time and adventures together. To a large extent, we did. She was my friend and faithful mother to our children. I worked to support her and keep us together. But like a lot of marriages, despite having been to seminars on this topic and knowing better, we slowly drifted apart and allowed blockades to exist that prevented a closer and stronger marriage.

I failed to meet her emotional needs for companionship, which caused her to seek it from the children. I felt excluded from the raising of the children, which caused me to give up and withdraw into my own work world. I'd let her do her thing and I'd do mine to avoid confrontation over how to raise the kids. The result of that was frequently, I felt like the "bad" guy in the family. I knew that she put the kid's needs above my own. They were right and I was wrong.

Likewise, my lack of involvement in the family life she saw as me withdrawing when I should be engaging. Due to my personality, when I latch onto something, I really latch onto it and focus. Pulling me away from it is hard. Combine that with a woman who needs attention and conversation, and you see where this is going. I had trouble paying attention to her so that she, over time, felt less and less loved by me. Not anything she consciously thought about, but a growing reality she buried by focusing on the children.

In the realm of sex, I felt she didn't love me as I had expected she would. From the first days of our marriage, what I expected was dashed to the ground. I had a strong sex drive and wanted that connection as frequently as possible. She was happy with three to four times a month. During the first five years of our marriage, that grew to a crisis level for me when it became even less. One year I began to doubt that she loved me because I felt she had rejected me.

I came to a decision concerning that when God sent me a clear message to wait, it would get better. So I waited, and over time she became more willing. But never more than averaging two to three times a month. The main change is she stopped avoiding it and welcomed that relationship with me, even though she didn't have the energy to actually think about it except on some weekends. It still wasn't a high priority on her list.

Despite that, I had come to a place of contentment after around year eight of our marriage. I didn't expect to get anything more on that front for the rest of our marriage. I'd gotten over the loss I felt in those first five years, though it was a real struggle for a while. I had accepted it as the way things were and no longer hoped or expected it to be different. I loved her, and was willing to sacrifice that for her.

So for the years leading up to October of 2010, we existed in this state of "truce" on these issues. They would occasionally pop up into a flare. She would want to talk with me, and my focus on my activities made it difficult to see what she was talking about as important. So she felt I thought she was unimportant. But I never saw that. I thought it was just a personality clash that happened occasionally. She was social and I was not, and that's just the way it was. So instead of doing something about it, instead of getting counseling to deal with it, we lived with it. We took each other for granted, existed in our own separate worlds, and moved on with life.

Problem was, however, these issues laid the groundwork for the temptation to come. We both felt we loved each other. At each anniversary, I'd ask her how she felt about our relationship, and she always said she felt good and happy about it and her life with me. We both felt strongly that we loved each other, and would be faithful to each other our whole lives. After 28 years of marriage, I didn't think there was a snowball's chance in Hell that our marriage would fall apart. Sure, we had issues, but didn't everyone? Compared to some, ours were minor indeed. We felt our love was strong, and anyone who knows me and my wife would tell you they would never have imagined she would do what she did.

As a matter of fact, I'd always feared if it happened, it would be me cheating on her, because I feared that possibility knowing my sex drive. I had this image of me losing my mind at some point and doing something stupid. Like going temporarily insane and coming out of it to realize you'd messed up your life and those around you over some moment of joy.

Perhaps that is why I didn't. I had that fear, so I'd built walls against it. Boundaries I wouldn't cross. Over the years, I'd had opportunities to cross them. I distinctly remember during the year-five crisis mentioned above, talking with a girl and realizing the intimate nature of the conversation, thinking to myself, "This is how affairs start! Warning! Back away from the woman!"

But by the time 2007 rolled around, my wife felt that she would never even so much as think of cheating on me. We both trusted each other explicitly. Even though she cleaned houses for some single men, I had no concern that she might do something inappropriate with them. Ironically, on that front, I was right. But the unresolved issues, not only in our marriage but with her need for attention, set her up so that a series of events presented her with the unthinkable: not only temptation to cheat, but the eventual wearing down of her walls and boundaries to commit the act.

Keep in mind, these things I've just described were marital issues.

They contributed to the degree of temptation she would experience once opportunity presented itself. In as much as I failed to address those issues or failed to even recognize them as issues, I played a part in the increase of her temptation. But these in no way excuse her for the decisions she made. I didn't cause her to cheat. She chose to deal with these issues by cheating.

That said, she didn't consciously make a decision at some point, "I'm dissatisfied with my marriage, I think I'll cheat." There are people who do consciously make that very decision, but for most who commit this act, they are more like someone who wanders too far into quicksand, and before they realize it, are in over their heads.

The following series of events shows how our pride and weaknesses can wear us down, even when we have strong morals and commitments, and think to ourselves, "I would never do that." When you think that, that's when you are the most vulnerable to do just that. Because then you fail to establish boundaries that prevent you from stepping into the quicksand.

If anything, the following should be a warning to anyone who thinks they would never cheat. My wife had strong morals against such a thing. For the longest time, she never dreamed she would ever cheat on me, even after she actually had emotionally. The following describes how someone can get worn down and give in to the marital sin of adultery. Read and take it to heart. This could be you if you don't take preventative measures. No one should assume they are safe.

The Set Up

At the time, we didn't see the events I'm about to outline as setting my wife up to be tempted to cheat. Understanding what happened has come through many sessions of self-examination and tracing out what brought my wife to the point of having an affair.

I will take this moment to praise my wife. In the days following what many in the support group call "D-day," that is, "discovery day," or the day I discovered her affair, my wife has been faithful to always talk about what happened, to answer my questions, as painful as I know it was for her at times. She never shied away from the painful process of cleaning the wound out of me.

Having been on a support group for the months since discovery day, I know how often the unfaithful spouse refuses to talk about the affair. Time and time again in those cases, the couple either continue in an unhappy marriage for years or it breaks up at some point. Why? Because the issues are buried and not dealt with. The wounds of the affair are covered up and left to fester instead of treated. The result is either to live with continuing pain or to eventually erupt into divorce.

For the hurt spouse, the need to acquire a clear picture of what happened isn't morbid curiosity, but a need to understand in the hopes of knowing how to heal. If you don't know why something happened, you can't figure out how to treat it. If you can't treat it, you know it is likely to happen again. Even if it doesn't, that is the constant fear. Until that fear is brought out into the open and dealt with, it will fester. Way too many unfaithful spouses want to avoid the painful topics and refuse to talk about them, which only prevents the wounds of the hurt spouse from healing.

But my wife never held back, no matter the question, no matter how painful or uncomfortable it was for her to discuss it. Truth be told, I think that fact is the main reason I healed as fast as I did, and why our marriage healed as well as it has. Because unless the pain is brought into the open instead of hidden, it cannot heal. A fact too often violated in the aftermath of an affair.

So a lot of what I'm about to lay out here is due to our examinations of what happened. It should be noted, none of this is definitive. These are our best evaluations of why she became susceptible to the temptation to cheat. Some of these we are pretty sure played a big role, others might have or might not have. Hard to determine, but I include them because it may have been a factor when taken together as a whole. But many people also face these situations and don't cheat. Because temptation arises, doesn't mean the tempted has no choice but to give in.

Need for Attention

I mentioned in the previous chapter that when I first met my wife as a teen, I saw her as an annoying teenager. She had a desperate need for attention and affirmation, no doubt arising from her childhood growing up in an emotionally distant, blended family of eight living in a very small house. So with friends, she tended to try too hard to be liked, causing her to be annoying instead.

When I came along, I solved that. Suddenly, here was a guy who loved her, paid lots of attention to her, and respected her, and wanted to spend his life with her. What could be more affirming than that? Then as kids came into the picture, she found her need for attention and love focused on them. They provided meaning to her life, while we as a couple grew farther apart.

So after over twenty-eight years of marriage, she thought the attention thing was something she'd fixed. She hadn't felt the need for attention and affirmation for a long time. But in reality, it lay under the surface. It was still there. It had been fed all those years first by me, and then by the kids. But the desire to be noticed, appreciated, and heard was still lingering in the background.

The Empty Nest

One of the factors that brought the above into play by 2010 was the reality that the kids were leaving home. Our youngest was in his junior year of high school, and getting ready for his senior year. Our oldest had already left home, living on her own, and was getting into a relationship with a man who would eventually become her husband. Our learning-disabled middle son would probably be around, but we were working toward helping him to become independent, and at some point in the future, live on his own.

By 2010, my wife became scared. Why? Because I hadn't paid her much attention over the past years, and as the kids would leave, all she saw for her immediate future was loneliness. Her fear was that she would sit around in her retirement years, doing whatever she could find to occupy her time, while I sat in my room working on my computer and rarely connecting with her.

She expressed this fear to me at least three times leading up to the affair. I dismissed it. I felt she was being too worried about something that wouldn't happen. I thought once the kids were out of the way, she'd be forced to put me back in the most-important-person-in-her-life slot. I was actually looking forward to it. I figured once she arrived there, she'd realize it wouldn't be as lonely as she feared. So I told her she was making a bigger deal out of it than it was and everything would be fine.

But in retrospect, she would have been right to a degree. If I had continued on that same course of interacting with her on minor occasions, I probably would have tended to ignore her a lot. While it is possible with the kids gone, the dynamic between us would have rejuvenated, and changed on its own, I can see how she would have felt it wouldn't. There wouldn't have been any compelling reason for me to do more than I was, and I wouldn't have likely changed much. She could have been very lonely as a result.

However, I was sure once we got to that point, she would be fine. It wouldn't be as bad as she thought. Whether that was true or not, however, didn't matter. The fact was, she feared that once the kids were gone, she'd be lonely and ignored by me. I did nothing to change that impression or give her a real reason to think otherwise.

The Lost Weight

During 2007, a big change happened in my wife's life. With each child she gave birth to, her weight had spiraled up and refused to come back down. After the third child, she was well over 200 pounds. She'd been that way through the biggest hunk of our marriage. Our first child was born in 1985 which put her over 200, and the last in 1993. So by 2007, she'd been overweight for 22 years of our then 25 years of marriage.

Keep in mind, I didn't bother her about this. I wanted her to lose weight for her health, but I was fully accepting of her as a person no matter how much she weighed. I wasn't the kind of guy who was that concerned about her looks as much as I was about her as a person. Like I said, what attracted me to her when we started dating was her personality, not her body. Though I need to add that her body wasn't bad either. It just wasn't what I felt was important in a person I loved.

When 2007 rolled around, I had come across a hypnosis program for losing weight. I thought it was funny, but she decided to check it out. As it ended up, it worked for her. All during 2007, she steadily dropped off the weight she'd been carrying around for most of our marriage. She lost around 87 pounds that year. We have a picture of her at the Christmas of 2006 and 2007 side-by-side, and the difference is huge. I was very happy for her. She had finally got a handle on it, and I felt she stood a better chance of living longer and not having some of the health problems often associated with being overweight.

However, I failed on one key point. I didn't rave over her weight loss. In part because I didn't want to make all the past few years of acceptance of her appear to be fake. I felt if I went, "Oh wow, honey! You look so hot now! Much better than you were before!" She would think I was only pretending to be okay with her weight before.

The truth was, I was okay as far as how I loved her and desired her. Sure, I wanted her to be healthier. If given a choice, fat or skinny, I would pick skinny. It wasn't a deal breaker for me, though. It wasn't what I felt was important from a desire-for-her standpoint. Therefore, I felt no need to start acting like I couldn't keep my hands off her. I loved her equally as much no matter what her weight was. Her losing weight didn't change how much I wanted her because that didn't factor into my desire for her.

But the event of her weight loss was a key attention need for her. She told everyone about it. She eagerly showed the side-by-side picture of her before and after. She told people at the convenience store, her clients, anyone who would listen. Why? She wanted the attention. She wanted people to go, "Wow! You really lost a lot of weight. Good job! You look great!"

I didn't give her that, but that's what she wanted. She started wearing tighter pants. She began sending out "I'm good looking" vibes because for the first time in her life, she felt sexy. Even though as a teen she was a lot skinner, back then she felt fat, even though she wasn't. I even tried to tell her she wasn't fat, but she wouldn't believe me. But by the end of 2007, for the first time in her life, she felt skinny and sexy.

Feeling sexier grew a more confident attitude. She began to send out the "I'm good looking" vibes, and men responded by flirting here and there. That attention made her feel even sexier.

By the time October of 2010 arrived, she'd been in this mode for around three years. We'd both gotten used to it. I didn't think much about it. I was happy she was skinnier, but failed to realize I had given her little attention and emotional support over it. So for three years, she'd gotten used to the idea that she could get that attention from other people, including other men who flirted with her from time to time. She'd grown to accept it as an innocent game she could play that stroked her attention-desiring passion.

Midlife Crisis

This is one element that is a little less important in the grand scheme of things, but we do feel it factored into it once the affair "fog" had settled in.

By way of definition, the "affair fog" refers to the mental mindset of someone who is cheating or is being drawn to cheat. It is called a fog because the person blocks out all concern for long term consequences in favor of immediate gratification. So mentally, they can't see more than a few inches past their nose, as if they were in a thick fog.

Once a person is in this fog, the human brain has this amazing capacity to convince itself why you should get what you want despite some very good reasons it should avoid it. So the following factor really only played into her mind once she was already neck deep in the quicksand, and the possibility of cheating on me no longer felt like something she'd never do. Or even before that, the desire had grown so much that it became a factor in her deteriorating resistance. One note: the "fog" isn't an excuse for having an affair. It only describes the mindset of someone involved in the addictive, infatuation-based desire of a new relationship.

Midlife crisis is somewhat of an ambiguous event. It is usually brought on by many factors and can be different for everyone. But it most often involves feelings of loss over dreams not accomplished, or events not shared in or achieved. A person arrives at the mid-point of their life, usually in their forties, and realizes they haven't done what they wanted to do. Where they saw themselves as they approached fifty-years-old isn't where they are at.

One of the factors in many women's midlife crisis involves the empty nest syndrome as we described above. But more generally not simply the feeling of loneliness, but of the change brought about when the children that a woman and man have invested their lives in for so many years are now leaving the house. Suddenly, their life changes just as drastically as when that first baby arrived in the hospital. For some women, their kids are their life. As they leave, meaning for life leaves with them, and they are left not merely feeling lonely, but lack purpose and desire. Often depression is the result, especially if menopause is a difficult time.

But for my wife, there was another element that factored into her demise once she'd played in the quicksand. That was the fact that for all her life, she'd never experienced any other man sexually than me. We'll see how this played into what happened more fully, but one of the feelings the first affair had sparked in her was a desire for experiences she'd never had. She began to feel like she'd missed out all her life on the joys everyone else was indulging in and enjoying. Her foggy brain convinced her she should have those experiences.

The Result

But that is jumping ahead a little. To back up, you can see where she was when October of 2010 flipped open on the calendar. She was feeling skinny and sexy, enjoying the attention she derived from others, including men willing to flirt with her. She was sending off confident, "I'm good looking" vibes for the first time in her life. She feared that I was so lost in my own world, as I had been for years by that point, that I would never give her the attention and love she wanted. So as the kids left the house, she only saw herself sitting alone if she relied on me for conversation and attention.

She had no reason to believe that the dynamic we'd had in place for well over twenty years would change in the next one or two years.

She had come to the point where the right opportunity would provide a temptation too strong for her to resist.

But temptation doesn't work so bluntly. If opportunity had popped up and offered for her to cheat, she wouldn't have taken it. Indeed, as we'll see in the next chapter, she resisted for several weeks. Rather, temptation works by getting its foot in the door, and slowly growing bigger and bigger. Like a frog in a pot that his heating up, you don't realize what is happening until it is too late.

No, the opportunity came through one man who latched onto my wife's signals of skinny, sexy, flirty, and therefore, he decided, available. Over a course of two months, he totally changed the personality of my wife.

Crossing Boundaries

Most spouses who end up cheating don't say to themselves, "My wife isn't meeting my needs. I think I'll go find someone who will." There are people who, because of their moral code, feel that cheating on one's spouse is expected and okay as long as you don't get caught. Some people are labeled "serial cheaters," in that they, for whatever reasons, have a history of being unfaithful with everyone and over many years. These kind of people can intentionally cheat on their wives.

But the majority doesn't go looking for it. Often I've heard from the unfaithful spouse, "I never thought I would ever cheat." For these people, it feels as if the affair just falls into their lap. Like a sudden, "It just happened before I realized it," thing. But for those not intending to have an affair, if they honestly evaluated what happened, they can usually mark key decisions they made which encouraged and supported the temptation rather than prevented it. Usually, the idea, "I would never do that," is what gives them boldness to take chances, to cross boundaries.

From stories I've heard, one common scenario is a man who goes to a bar when away from home, maybe with friends or co-workers, and once drunk, does something he wouldn't have done while sober. Which may or may not be true, but that's the story. If true, and he knew he does "stupid things" when he is drunk, by going to a bar with attractive women and drinking until drunk, he crossed boundaries he knew he shouldn't cross. On the surface, these things can seem innocent. "Lots of people go to bars and don't have sex with someone while there. Why can't I go have a drink with my friends?" But for him, he knew he was playing with fire. Crossing that boundary set him on the path to cheat and was part of his decision to cheat.

Other common boundaries described are two co-workers that start discussing intimate marital problems they are having. Flirting. Spending more time with someone other than your spouse. Allowing opportunities that could lead to temptation to exist, like staying after hours to work with the boss, leaving you and her the only two there. Making inappropriate remarks. The list could go on.

My wife crossed some of these as well. She thought she could "handle it." She seriously believed she would never cheat on me, but even while thinking that, she was taking her first steps to do exactly that. Here are the boundaries she crossed, and how each step led her deeper and deeper into the quicksand of her passions.

Flirting

As I mentioned in the last chapter, my wife enjoyed the attention that men gave her after she lost weight and started wearing tighter clothing to show off her new figure. For the first time since early in our marriage, she started wearing jeans again. I would catch her staring at her body in the mirror, checking out her clothes and appreciating the way she looked.

As stated, she was ripe for opportunity to come knocking. It did in the form of a redneck man that I'll call Clyde, which is not his real name. He actually used an animal name as a nickname, but any alternative I could think of would sound like I was intending to be degrading. So we'll go with Clyde just to be nice.

Clyde was hired by a company in the spring of 2010. My wife cleaned their building once every week. When she first saw Clyde, she thought he was "adorable." She had an immediate attraction to him.

But as it turned out, Clyde had a very loose moral code when it came to having sex. He had a live-in-girlfriend, but apparently she wasn't providing his needs as he wanted, and he had no qualms about going outside of their relationship to get it. So when he encountered my wife with her sexy attitude, it drew him to her.

For several months, he mostly flirted with her. She would say something like, "Can you turn on that light for me?" He might respond, "Sure, I'd love to turn you on." She said he regularly turned everything she said into a sexual remark. At first, this was it, and my wife took it as nothing more than a fun game. He gave her attention, and she enjoyed it. But in allowing him to engage her in this manner, by indicating pleasure at his statements rather than disapproval, she crossed a boundary. It seemed innocent to her, but for him, it indicated he could go further.

Giving Him Her Number

After this had gone on for around six months, in early October of 2010, he gave her his card, and told her to text him sometime if she liked. In essence, he wanted her phone number and was testing to see if she was willing. She'd never had a man pursue her like that before, so to her the request felt innocent enough. But when a man asks for your phone number, they are asking permission to go further with you. So she texted him within minutes of him giving it to her. She'd established personal contact with him outside of her work.

Bottom line, married women don't give out their phone number to men short of a strictly business relationship. He wasn't asking for her to come clean his house. He only had one thing in mind, and it wasn't business.

But she liked him and liked his attention. Him wanting her phone number was another level of attention. But when she decided to give it to him, she crossed another boundary by sending him the signal that it was okay for him to privately contact her.

Sex-texting

After he had her phone number, a week later he texted her some flirts a couple of times. She still saw this as just a fun game she enjoyed as had been going on for months because she liked the attention he was giving her.

She even told me about him flirting with her via text. I told her that it was not a good idea. That guys when they flirt aren't playing a game—that they take flirting back as a sign you want more. That you are serious. It was inappropriate for a married woman to be sending those signals to another man. She confessed this to our priest, who also warned her to stop the flirting and cut it off with this guy.

But she was already in the pull of an affair. By giving him her number and responding positively to his advances, she developed an inappropriate relationship with him. She convinced herself it was all for fun and games. Nothing serious. She felt she would never do anything to cheat on me. Problem was, by ignoring my wishes and our priest's warnings, she actually already had done that. She quickly fell into the quicksand of the passions.

Around mid-October, Clyde sent what would be the first of many sex-texts. At first, she was shocked when she received such a message from him. But she passed it off as part of the game. She responded as if innocent and not catching the sexual message.

The next day, he sent another sex-text. This one made her realize, for the first time, that he was serious about wanting to do the sexual activities he was describing. For the first time in her life, a man other than me was serious about wanting to have sex with her. That had never happened to her before. The feelings it sent through her attention-desiring mind was the equivalent of a high from a drug. An excitement flooded her, and she wanted more of it. I couldn't give her that high, but this man could.

The orgasmic-like feelings of pleasure that raced through her upon realizing he really wanted to do these things to her, sucked her deep into a fantasy fog at that moment. She literally became another person. Because of that reaction, she rationalized to herself the crossing of another boundary. She responded positively to his sex-text. She said to herself, "Let's find out where this will go." She wrote a text back to him of like kind, and hit send.

If there is one point where I could say the affair officially went into high gear, it was at this point. Why? Because, one, it is very obvious that sex-texting with someone other than your spouse is way out of bounds. Two, she knew it because from that point on she didn't tell me about the sex-text, or that they were communicating, and she stopped talking to me about him at all.

What arose at this point was the beginning of compartmentalization. This is a process where a person lives two or more different lives, with different personalities, and realities. To bring the two lives together would force her to decide between them, but by dividing them in her mind, she was able to hold onto both. This began that process, and it grew to epic proportions as she went further and further down that road.

Mentally, she felt like inside of her were two people. She labeled them "bad girl" and "good girl." These two persons inside of her began fighting. Early on, good girl won most of the fights. For example, when she received that second sex-text from him and responded, she still felt it was a game, and not serious on her part. But she now realized he was taking it seriously. So she approached him the next time she cleaned at the business and made it clear that she was happily married to me and would under no circumstances ever do any of the things they had described in their texts.

This cooled him off for a few days after he agreed and understood. But obviously her desire for his attention caused him to realize he still had a chance to wear her down. So he started back to sex-texting her.

Bad girl won small victories like this, in that instead of her refusing to participate, she rationalized that he knew she would never do any of it, he now knew it was just a game to her, and she could continue participating in that game since it was clear she wouldn't cheat on me. Despite the fact she was doing it already.

Her (and I as well) didn't think of such things as cheating. We thought that only happened when sex happened. But having an affair is much more involved than simply having sex. Sharing any intimacy of a martial nature with another person is cheating. Sex-texting with another man definitely falls into that category. Bottom line: if you feel a need to hide it from your spouse, it is cheating.

Despite not knowing what was going on other than that this man was flirting with her, all I knew was she had suddenly gone from wanting sex a couple of times a month on the average, to wanting it as often and frequently as she could get it. It was like someone had flipped a switch on that had been off all those years. There was only one other time when she acted that way, and that was when she'd read a romance book, which she hadn't done in years. But in essence, I figured that was what was happening. His flirting with her had fired off her desire for sex, and I was the beneficiary of the event.

If I had known what was really going on, I would have been more concerned. Truth be told, I did have concerns. I realized she was more attached to this man than she should be. But three things kept me from seriously investigating at this point.

One, I was enjoying the amount of sex I had wished I had through our whole marriage, but never received except in short bursts. I figured this too would die off within a month, and I might as well enjoy it while I had it. Because it never lasted long.

Two, I had always trusted her implicitly. I felt it would be a cold day in Hell before she would cheat on me. So when she assured me nothing more than the flirting had happened, I believed her. I never considered it necessary to pick up her phone while she slept to search her texts, or check the phone bill to see a common phone number popping up that was strange.

Three, I was so ensconced in my own world of writing and hated to be interrupted, that I didn't have much interest and energy to invest in thinking about why she suddenly wanted sex so much. In October, I was deep in writing a series of chapters, getting nine stories done in eight weeks. I was spending late nights focused on that, and then in November on the "National Novel Writing Month," where writers from all over the world work to write fifty thousand plus words on a novel in the month of November, that I simply didn't have time to digest what was going on with her. As usual, I was so focused on my world that I didn't have time for hers.

So for two months straight, she was free to do what she wanted without me getting in the way. He and her played this sex-texting "game" until mid-December of 2010. That's when she crossed a big boundary, that led to her first major physical affair.

Secret Meeting

Come mid-December, she came to me and announced that Clyde was leaving town in a week, departing for Mississippi by the next Wednesday. Part of me rejoiced. By this time, I knew she was way too connected to him for my comfort level. But I still didn't know the extent of it. She only admitted to flirting with him. But the reality of it was the two months of sex-texting with him had strengthened bad girl at good girl's expense. Even though she still told herself she would never have sex or do anything sexual with him, she found herself wishing she could.

But another part of me feared him leaving. Because though she assured me that she hadn't done anything sexual with him, knowing her attachment to him, the desire to meet him and give in I knew would be strong that coming week, as she would see it as her last chance to do so. So I told her under no circumstances was she to meet him anywhere or talk to him before he left town. I knew the temptation would be too great if that happened.

Unfortunately, I was prophetic, and she didn't listen to me. She and Clyde agreed to meet at an outdoor fast-food type restaurant, where you order from a speaker like a Sonic Drive-in. They met on Wednesday, in another town, two days before he was to leave. They parked at the end of a row with no other cars around, and he sat in her car, they ordered, and ate. Without going into detail, the one thing he'd always asked her to do was oral sex. She gave in and did it.

He left and headed back to continue to prepare for his move. She drove back to our town thinking, "I can never tell Rick about this." For the first time in her life, she'd committed a physical, sexual act with another man than me. A major boundary had been crossed. It was at this point that she realized this was not a game anymore. It had become real. She had cheated even by her more liberal definition of the word.

Bad girl had won a big victory at this point. Now she'd crossed a major boundary, and what followed would come easier. She'd done something she thought she'd never do. Once that happens, everything is fair game.

That said, good girl won a final battle. The last one she would win until discovery day. Unknown to me, for she never told me this until after discovery day, Clyde made another trip to town to get the rest of his stuff about a week after he had left. When he arrived, he contacted my wife, told her he would be free that Wednesday, and would like to have her come to his trailer. It so happened that she didn't have a client Wednesday afternoon, so she had the time to do it. She texted back to him that fact.

Part of her really wanted to meet him, because she really wanted to have sex with him. She knew this would be her one and only chance. Being so infatuated with him to the point of irrationality, she knew what would happen if she went.

But this also scared her. At the previous meeting, she didn't think she would do anything like what she did. That she did it took her by surprise. She thought she had the strength and character not to give in to the desire. But now she knew better. She knew she would cross the final boundary of intercourse if she met with him.

So in a moment of "good girl clarity," being afraid of what would happen if she went, she arranged to meet me for lunch that Wednesday. When that day rolled around, we met and ate at a local restaurant. Clyde kept texting her, trying to convince her to come and see him before time ran out.

Lunch ended and we were leaving. She knew if we parted ways, she'd still have time to go meet him and the worst would happen. So at the last minute she asked me if I wanted to go home and have sex. I agreed (luckily), and by the time we were done, it was too late, and Clyde had given up.

Clyde left town two days later. They texted a few times, but didn't try to meet up again. We've never seen nor heard from him since. I didn't know how close she'd come to taking that final step in cheating. While good girl had won a victory, it actually planted the seed for ultimate defeat since she regretted not having had sex with him. Her desire for him grew even though she would never see him again.

Boundaries had been crossed that set the stage for what was to come, and the final boundary falling as well, sexual intercourse.

Living the Fantasy

I relaxed once I knew Clyde was gone. Her seeming attachment to him made me uncomfortable, even though I thought nothing had happened between them other than some flirting via text. But I felt now that he was gone, the danger had passed and she would slowly forget him and get back to normal. I couldn't have been more wrong.

Likewise, she too thought it was over. She'd made some serious mistakes, and committed one sexual act with another man, but at least she'd not had sexual intercourse with him. She too thought she would get over him, life would get back to normal, and she could keep what happened safely in the past, something I would never have to find out about, and something she was unlikely ever to repeat again.

This is an outlook common to unfaithful spouses once the affair has ended and the spouse never discovered it. They often feel they can bury it in the past. They learned their lesson. Don't hurt the spouse by telling them about it. Go on as if nothing had happened, and life will go back to normal, no one is the worse for wear.

The problem with this approach is that it rarely ever works out that way. If an unfaithful spouse wishes to continue his marriage after such an event, he usually ensure the loss of the marriage by doing so. One of the chapters in the next part of this book deals with the frequent question from unfaithful spouses in situations like this: Should I Tell? Outside of some narrow instances, the answer is usually, "Yes."

One of the reasons I suggest as to why an unfaithful spouse should tell applies to my wife's situation. As long as the secret exists, the motivation to cheat is not effectively dealt with and the likelihood of a repeat affair goes way up. She thought it was over, she would get over him in time, and life would go back to "normal." But by not confessing to me what had happened, there was no motivation to fix what had gone wrong. So it continued to fester in her. Instead of getting over him, her desire for him grew, and a longing for what she'd missed out on. If she would have confessed then what had happened, chances are it would have ended with that one man. But because she didn't, he was not the last one. She remained deep in desire, infatuation, and what we call, "the fog" created when the passions drive one's decisions.

So the following is a standard example of what happens when one says to herself, "It's over. I won't make that mistake again. I can handle it. He never needs to know that I cheated on him. It would only hurt him." Here's what happens when one fails to throw water on the fire of an affair through confession.

Online Activity

Clyde had left town for good just past midway in December of 2010. We went through Christmas that year, and she still acted very much not herself. She constantly talked about "bad girl" and "good girl" in her desires. She still wanted sex as often as possible. But I thought this would all soon die down as her infatuation with this man died off.

The problem was, her infatuation with him didn't die off. I realized that one day in mid-January of 2011 when I happened to look over her shoulder to see her cell phone screen. She usually had a picture of me for her wall paper. But when I looked that time, I saw a picture of Clyde, a month after he'd left. That was bad enough, but I could tell by her reaction when she noticed I'd seen it, quickly shifting the picture away back to my picture and the guilty look on her face, that her infatuation with him was still strong.

The uneasy feeling returned, and I didn't like the idea that she had his picture on her phone. I expressed that to her, and she promised to remove it. But that did little to dampen her feelings for him. I say, "feelings for him," but in reality it was her feelings for the experience he provided. It really wasn't so much Clyde she wanted, but the feelings he generated in her. But she'd attached to the two as one, and so wanted him.

This lead her to start seeking him out. He had pretty much broken the connection with her. He'd changed his phone number and never told her the address he'd moved to. He was the kind that once he'd made his mark, he moved on and didn't want any kind of relationship. He was only after the sex, and nothing else. But Lenita went online and did a search on him. She came up with an address. Not much but it was a connection. She saved the info in expectation when his birthday rolled around, she would send him a card to surprise him.

She also recalled that Clyde had a MySpace account. He'd told her that he never looked at it. He wasn't the social networking type, but at one point someone had convinced him to create an account. So she decided to create an account at MySpace as well and friend him. Her idea was if and when he ever looked at his account, there her friend request would be, and he might reestablish contact with her. So she set it up early February, friended Clyde, and then waited.

As anyone who has a MySpace account knows, one gets lots of friend request from people who want to sexually play. They usually want to sex chat, or have you look at their porn site, or do phone sex, any number of activities. When these request started coming through both friend request and her private messages, and being she was in the fog of the affair with Clyde, these were like beacons of temptation shining brightly on a dark, lonely night while missing Clyde and what he provided.

She started responding to some of these requests and messages around mid-February of 2011. It didn't take long for her to discover there were a good number of people willing to have the same type of sex chats and fun as she's had with Clyde. At this point, it began to dawn on her that she didn't need Clyde to get the same rush of excitement. Any guy would do. Plus, online contacts seemed safer than local people she knew. She developed online relationships with two men on MySpace, and several minor contacts with others. Those two relationships would continue until I discovered her affairs.

She even went so far with one of these men to have a phone sex session. One of the men didn't live too far away, and it was only because he was dirt poor and couldn't afford the gas that he didn't drive to our town. Because even though she said she didn't want or intend to encourage him, she nearly begged for him to come so she could "have that experience" she missed out on with Clyde.

But MySpace wasn't enough. She wanted more. So she did some searching and found a site that shared "experiences" of all types. One of the experiences they shared a lot on there was of a sexual nature. Fantasy stories, pictures, what they enjoyed or didn't enjoy, etc. Yet, the big bonus for her is she met several guys online that she enjoyed chatting with, usually about sexual topics.

She enjoyed one man in particular. He claimed to be a writer of erotica novels. He wanted to use her to help write one of his stories about a house cleaning worker since she cleaned houses. He would give her scenarios and ask her what she would do, would like done to her, or not, and he could write his story based on her responses.

Upon hearing of this after the fact, my guess is he probably didn't write novels. That was his way of sex chatting with women. Whether he told the truth or not, she had developed online contacts with several men through this site and MySpace, and now spent most of her spare time at home on the computer. Oddly enough, the computer was in the living room, and usually the kids were in there. Though they saw her pop another screen up quickly when she was aware they looked, they didn't think anything about it. Also she often stayed on the computer until one or two in the morning. Being that I tended to be on my computer in our bedroom most of the time, it was easy when I came walking down the hall for her to flip over to another screen as I walked by.

Her new interest in spending time on the computer did stand out to me. I also thought it strange, because for our whole marriage, she'd avoided spending a lot of time on the computer once we had one, and no matter what she was doing, she easily fell asleep. She usually had to go to bed by midnight, as she could barely keep herself awake long enough to get ready for bed. When she hit the pillow, she was out. Now, by some unknown miracle, she was staying up until two in the morning, typing away at the computer.

It seems stupid now, looking back in retrospect, that I didn't wonder or suspect something at this point. What she was doing was totally out of character for her. But as I've noted before, I was focused in my own world.

One night when it was nearing two in the morning, I noticed she still had not come to bed. I realized this had become a normal occurrence and how weird it was. My reaction? I laughed that she had somehow become more like me, working on things late into the night. After all, she still was not her old pre-Clyde self. One more oddity among many didn't raise any red flags. She no longer watched the shows she'd always watched before. Instead, her new interest was online. I never wondered what she was doing that kept her so energized at it. I brushed it off and focused on my own work.

By mid-March, she was fully engaged in this online sex-chat world. What this activity did was to pretty effectively put good girl in a closet, then shut and lock the door. By spending time with this sex-crazed crowd, she started believing that sex outside of marriage wasn't an unthinkable act. She still held to a boundary of no physical sex, but due to her cyber-play, more and more the idea of having sex with someone other than me didn't sound like forbidden fruit. Rather, without her noticing it, her "innocent fun" fed the desire for such an experience that she'd never had.

So when opportunity came knocking again, "good girl" didn't have a fighting chance. That opportunity arrived in mid-March.

Falling in Love

My oldest son signed up for a gym membership. Shortly after that, in the first part of March, Lenita also signed up for the gym and they went together. She asked me to come as well. Little did I know if I had said "yes," it would have totally changed the course of future events. But though I knew I needed the exercise, I couldn't see taking time away from my writing to go work out, something I wasn't that excited about doing anyway. Rather, I saw it as another time slot when I could work on my writing without being interrupted by anyone. I couldn't pass that up to go "waste" my time punishing my body. So I said no, and she and my son started going to the gym regularly.

By this time, Lenita was sending out "sexy" signals pretty strong. The gym provided plenty of opportunity to show off her body. Within a week or two of her attending the gym, a man showed up. Like the other man, we'll not use his real name, and call him Bubba. As my wife was to learn a bit later, and me much later, Bubba's brother had paid for his gym membership with the idea he could find himself a woman by going there. So he was on the prowl, and my wife was broadcasting available signals.

It started out by him using the elliptical exercise machine next to her. He struck up a conversation. My wife, being the sociable type and subconsciously looking for experiences herself, started talking with him. It wasn't long before they'd struck up a friendship. She even told me about meeting this man the first day. I nodded and went on with my business. However, their friendship progressed quickly when she invited him to swim with her in the pool. She started spending time with him outside of the gym. She took him to buy a swimming suit, shoes, and before you knew it, anytime she went to the store, whether grocery shopping, buying items for a client, or office store, she would call him and he would meet her there.

My son thought they were just friends. They were careful not to do anything obvious in public, but when they thought they could get away with it, they would hold hands. With good girl effectively out of commission, and spending so much time together, in a mere two weeks, he took her in his car to a remote location to have sex. She knew it was going to happen, but by this point, she had little to no resistance to the idea. Toward the end of March 2011, my wife, for the first time in her life, had sexual intercourse with a man other than me.

Lenita at first battled what had happened. She knew it wasn't good. Good girl opened the closet door a crack, and she tried to break it off with Bubba. However, her heart wasn't in it, and no sooner had she said, "We can't continue with this," than it continued. By the second time they had sex, she literally gave up on the idea of fighting it. In her mind, it was happening, there was nothing she could do, so she might as well go with the flow and stop fighting.

She ended up falling in love with him. Not in the infatuation way she "loved" Clyde. That was totally sex driven, desire driven, and her desire for him was totally irrational. She knew it, but didn't care. She wanted him even though she knew for him she was nothing more than a sex object, a conquest. But Bubba was not as "adorable" as Clyde was. She wasn't even immediately attracted to him when he first showed up in the gym. But what Bubba did do was fill the holes I had failed to fill. He spent time with her. She had him help her on cleaning jobs when needed. Even in sex, while he didn't give her what I did, provided her with feelings she didn't get from me.

So as the weeks started piling up, she developed a real love and caring for Bubba, and by all accounts, him for her as well. It wasn't so much a love built on desire and passion, as it was with Clyde, but one built on companionship. The sex came along with the package.

It wasn't that she had stopped loving me either. As a matter of fact, she told him if I ever found out, that it would be over between them. That she could never leave me and she would chose me over him. But they hoped they could keep it going for several months at least before it came to an end.

She had by that point come to the conclusion she could love two men. One of them provided what the other did not. It appeared to be "working." She was deep in an affair in all ways possible. She'd had "emotional" affairs with several men both online and in person. She had the equivalent of a one-night sexual affair. Now she'd had a full long-term, falling in love, emotional and physical affair, going all the way.

Their affair lasted for around six weeks, from late March through

May 11, 2011. Then we're back where this story started. May 11th. The day I discovered my wife had cheated on me, multiple times. How did I find out and what happened then? That is the subject of the next chapter.

The Aftermath of Truth

Up to this point, I had brushed off all the red flags I had seen as either nothing to worry about or the last gasps of whatever connection she may have had with Clyde. I trusted my wife implicitly. When she said nothing was going on, I believed her. It never even registered on my radar screen that she might be lying and that I needed to check up on her. After all, we'd been married for almost 29 years. We had three wonderful children, mostly grown up, but two still living with us. In that time, my wife had never cheated, acted at all interested in other men, or lied to me about something so critical to the health of our relationship.

Yet that was exactly what was going on. So what caused me to finally get suspicious enough to start checking, and how did I find out? And the big question, what happened after that? This chapter explores the first two questions and the immediate aftermath of the discovery.

The Suspicions

Sunday, May 8, 2011. I was passing through the living room. My wife was at the computer, as usual. She was not aware I stood behind her. I decided to poke my head over her shoulder as if checking what she was looking at. Mostly as a joke. I didn't even look at the computer screen. I was just going for the "jump" reaction.

I got a different kind of reaction. She'd been chatting on her sex-chat site. When I scared her, she jumped, but also quickly Shift-Tabbed away from the screen she was on. Not having seen what she was looking at, I wondered what she wanted to hide from me. But I didn't push it. I figured it was some little secret she'd reveal to me later. After all, our anniversary was coming up the next weekend. I figured she was looking online to order me a gift and didn't want me to see what she was considering.

So I laughed at her and headed back to my bedroom to continue my writing tasks for that evening. If that was all that had happened, that would probably be where it ended, like so many other red flags I had dismissed. But something followed on the heels of that event that caused me to start connecting the dots and to investigate further.

Monday, May 9, 2011. We were both in our bedroom. She was getting ready for bed while I was looking over the cell phone bill, getting ready to pay it. We had a family plan, so all our phone details were on the bill.

What I didn't know is that the phone detail contained a lot of calls to a particular number. She regularly called and texted Bubba, sometimes talking for hours. But I rarely looked over the phone bill with that much detail to notice particular phone numbers. This time was no different.

What I did notice, however, is that she had sent and received an unusually large number of multi-media messages. To translate what that means for those not familiar with the term, those are messages sent with attached pictures and/or video. Our phone bill separates those out from the regular text messages.

Not that I expected to find anything other than maybe she'd sent some picture to our daughter who lived in a near-by town, but I decided to look at the numbers. If that was all I had done, I would have seen a few strange numbers. She does have clients and could have sent them pictures of what she'd cleaned or something she found broken, etc. I probably wouldn't have given it much thought.

But what did catch my attention is that she had texted three media messages to email addresses that were listed on the bill. Two of those email addresses contained men's names. Names I didn't know. Unknown to me at the time, one of them was Bubba. I couldn't figure out who these men were and why she'd be sending them pictures. So, I asked, "Who are David and Bubba?"

Silence. I didn't even look at her. I was staring at the bill. I'd caught her off guard, and she didn't know what to say, so she said nothing. When she didn't respond with an, "Oh, those are two clients I was sending pictures to for…," but remained quiet, not answering my question, I thought to myself, "This isn't good."

By her reaction, I knew something was up. I began to connect the dots. She's been on the computer a lot, she didn't want me to see what she was doing on the computer the night before, and she can't answer who those men were that she'd sent pictures too. It was then that I noticed one number popping up frequently in the picture message list as well. I had no idea to whom she was sending pictures, and what those pictures were. But I began to realize there was the distinct possibility she was involved with sex chats online.

Even then, with that sinking feeling, I didn't do anything immediately until the next evening. I let the subject drop, and didn't bring it up. I didn't even check to see if those numbers appeared regularly in the phone bill, which I would have found out they did quite a number of times. Instead, I decided to think about it. I almost filed it away and dismissed yet another red flag.

I know, I know. Crazy, right? But one of the first stages of grief when confronted with something of this nature is denial. You don't want to admit it is or has happened, and will look for any explanation that will reconcile it as an innocent misunderstanding. I had to give my mind some time to decide how to handle this. I had options. But I don't process information very quickly. So I let it simmer and didn't think too much more about it that evening.

God's Hand

Before we get any further, we should back up a bit and let you in on what had been happening on her side. Even though she'd justified her affair, inside she knew what she was doing was wrong. She would have what she called, "moments of clarity." This is when she saw clearly what she was doing and panicked over it. She knew that she was risking our marriage and was hurting me and the kids.

It was such a moment of clarity that caused her to try and break it off with Bubba, but failed. In other moments of clarity, she'd feel helpless to stop it or get out of it, and would simply offer up a prayer to God, "Save me from myself."

May 8, 2011, she had one of those moments of clarity while in the church service. She prayed, "God, save me from myself."

You see, God heard. He worked this out so precisely that she had no choice but to come clean about everything. I mean, everything. I know for those who don't believe in God, the following will seem like simply some fortunate circumstances that happened to strike at the same time. That's fine. I'm not here to convert anyone. But my belief is that God heard and arranged it to fully out her. She'd come to the conclusion she couldn't stop it. But God could provide her some real motivation to do so.

Keep this in mind as you read the following.

The Discovery

Tuesday, May 10, 2011. I'd gone to work the following day after the big red flag had been raised that I couldn't ignore very easily. Who were these men? Why did she clam up when I asked her who they were? Her reaction when I asked worried me most. She acted guilty, as if she couldn't tell me who they were, and wasn't prepared to lie.

Most of the day as I worked, I forgot about it. I really didn't think much about it until that evening. I'd come home from work a little before 6:00, and as usual, went to my room to do my writing tasks. Lenita was working unusually late that evening, because she had a big house to clean. Unknown to me, her affair partner was cleaning it with her and they'd had sex earlier that day before they left to clean. But she wasn't expected to get home until close to 8:00.

While in my room, my mind returned to the reaction I received from her the night before. My suspicions returned, and I began to wonder what was up. There were only two ways I might find out.

One was to simply confront her and press her to tell me what was going on. While I've heard some suggest this route, and for some that may be the only route, I'm glad I didn't take it. I wouldn't have found out the full scope of what was going on if I had. She'd already decided in her mind weeks before that if I found out about the online activity, she'd hide the affair she was having. My suspicions were that it was an online sex activity, and if that is what she ended up confessing to, I would have thought that was it and not discovered the full truth.

The problem is, most people having an affair will lie to their spouse about it. In their minds, what you don't know, won't hurt you. They don't think, "I am hurting him," they think, "If he ever finds out, then I've hurt him." But the reality is not only has the hurt spouse already been hurt at the point the affair started and continues, but the real reason the unfaithful spouse doesn't want to tell is because they don't want to deal with the consequences of what they've done. As long as the spouse doesn't know they're hurt, the unfaithful spouse doesn't have to face the truth of their infidelity.

I innately knew this as well. It was obvious she was hiding something from me. That meant she wouldn't be forthcoming or would be likely to explain away things. Indeed, I figured if I asked her then, after a whole day had passed, she'd probably already had cooked up a good story to tell me about why those men's email addresses received pictures from her, and how it was all nothing.

I knew if I wanted to find out the truth, I would need to investigate. Being she used one computer, and I figured mostly what she was doing was the online sex chats, a key logger would be the answer.

I debated it for a few minutes. Part of me wanted to just forget it and go about my writing. Our anniversary was only four days away. Did I want something like that hanging over my head? That I had to secretly spy on my wife? I wanted to believe it was just nothing, and my mind was being overactive. However, I couldn't shake the feeling that something was wrong. I needed to get to the bottom of this.

So I decided before she came home that evening that I would install a key logger on her computer. I did the Internet searches, found one that looked decent. It had a trial, so I decided I would install it for the length of the trial and hope that within the trial period, I would find out all I needed to know. I expected to be recording her chats up until we left for our anniversary trip. But as it turned out, I didn't have to wait any longer than a few hours to find out the full truth.

I installed the key logger, and then went back to my room to wait. As the evening wore on, she came home, we ate, and we both, as usual, sat in our separate rooms working on our separate tasks. Me with my writing, her with her sex chats. It was around 2:00 am when she finally came to bed and fell asleep. Once I felt confident she had gone solidly to sleep, I slipped into the living room, opened the key logger program, and found the recorded log.

I opened it up and began reading. As stated in the beginning of this book, I quickly discovered my suspicions were correct. She was participating in sexual conversations with other men in a social media site I'll leave unnamed. No, not Facebook. Though she did have some conversations there recorded between her and her affair partner. But I don't want to advertise the site, so we'll leave it at that.

Keep in mind what I said in the previous section. Up to this point, she'd never discussed her local affair with anyone online, fearing it might get back to me. She didn't plan on doing so. But God was at work. If she hadn't spilled the beans that night or in the next few nights, it is highly possible I would have thought that the online activity was the extent of it, and believed her when she confirmed that. But God had other plans.

The second man she talked to in the log was mentioned earlier. The one who told her he was writing an erotica novel about a housekeeper, and was using my wife as the "model" for what his character did. He'd also related to her and others on the site that he was in a sexless marriage. His wife didn't want sex with him at all, period, end of story. So he said. My suspicion is none of that was true and it was his way of beginning the conversation to attempt to meet up with my wife for an affair. But his story was that he'd put up with it for years, and was breaking down and deciding he was going to have an affair. He had to get some sex.

His confession, whether true or not, emboldened Lenita to confess to him that she was in the middle of an affair. That she'd had sex that morning with him. That it had been going on for weeks, and he cleaned houses with her, and that she'd committed a non-intercourse sexual act with Clyde back in December. She spilled out all of this, including what she liked about sex with me and Bubba, and how each fulfilled what she wanted in its own way.

As I stated at the beginning, this revelation floored me. I expected the sex chat. I didn't expect to find that she had cheated with Clyde, and was currently cheating with a man under my nose. It totally blew me away, because throughout our marriage I thought I would always know when something was bothering her. She couldn't hide it. If she was angry or frustrated, it just bubbled up to the surface. I was sure if anything of this nature was going on with her, there would be no way she'd be able to act like everything was okay. I thought her guilt would crush her.

So when I sat in the chair after reading the log, I said to myself, "I don't know her anymore." She'd changed. At that moment, I felt I had lost her. My first assumption was she didn't love me. How could anyone do this and love their spouse? I didn't know about compartmentalization. I didn't know about her giving into addictive desires. I didn't know she rationalized that she could love two people at the same time. All I knew was for the first time in our lives, she'd brought another man into our marriage. She'd joined as one with another. Multiple times.

I must have stayed up until 4:00 that morning of May 11th. I went through a lot of emotions during that time, but the biggest was uncertainty. About a lot of things. Uncertain how she could have reached this state and me not notice. Uncertain whether she still really loved me or not. Uncertain whether we would make it to our 30th anniversary just over a year away, much less get past the one in four days. Also, I was uncertain about all the resulting fall out for our family if this ended our marriage. Especially with a daughter planning on getting married the next year, and our son graduating from high school a month after that. Would we be attending those events as divorced parents? If not that, in a miserable marriage?

The pressing concern was also the big trip we had planned to take over the weekend. Friday was our anniversary. Did I cancel the reservations and stay home now? When should I confront her about it? Or should I just quietly put her away? Would I ever be able to trust her again? If we tried to rebuild, would we be able to do it successfully? Would she give up the other man?

So many thoughts whirled through my head. I finally decided if I was going to be functioning at work the next day, if I could, I needed some sleep. So I finally made my way back to the bedroom, knowing getting to sleep might be impossible. But all that I had processed had left me drained, not to mention I was up late in the morning.

When I entered the bedroom and saw her sleeping on the bed, I whispered, "How can you sleep, knowing what you are doing?" But there she was, snoring away, oblivious to the fact that I now knew everything. If there was more, it couldn't be much worse. She'd already confessed to the worst.

But the thought that continued to haunt me, and would for several days, is the unbelief that it had happened. I didn't want to believe it. I hoped when I talked to her, she might say something like, "Oh yeah, I noticed you put a key logger on my computer, so I decided to teach you a good lesson." Though that would have been ultra mean, I would have rather had that be the truth.

I went to sleep that night, knowing my life, my marriage, and my relationship with my wife would never be the same again. Whatever happened, what we had in our marriage was history. From that point on, when I saw a photo or a dated letter, email, or other item, my mind would immediately categorize it as pre-affair and post-affair. When I looked at a photo of us on a previous anniversary, I would think, "If only I'd known then what was coming." That marriage of innocence and absolute trust in one another was dead. What was to replace it is where the uncertainty came into the picture. Everything was up in the air. The future, even in the next few days, could go any number of different directions.

The only thing I felt I knew at all, is that God knew, and it was in His hands.

The Confrontation

The next morning, I began the process of unraveling the uncertainty. My first step was to call my priest. He returned my call at work, and I related to him what had happened. His first question to me was, "Do you want a divorce?"

I hadn't even considered it much. But obviously he had to ask that question to find out where I was at. A lot of people mistakenly believe that when Jesus said that divorce is committing adultery except in the case of infidelity, that what Jesus really meant was if your spouse cheats on you, you should divorce that person. Likewise, some people believe that Jesus was giving a "get out of jail free" card if your spouse had cheated on you. I suppose if our marriage had been horrible, and I no longer loved her, that might have been a real option.

However, I loved my wife. Even though she'd done what she did. Some may think I'm crazy for doing so. Yet, I think people don't tend to know what love really is. They mistake infatuation—what makes me feel good about him or her—as the essence of what love is. But the feelings will rise and fall. If one's love for another is attached to those feelings, their love will rise and fall with them. So people report "falling out of love" as if they accidentally fell off a cliff. I'll go into more detail about love in part 4, but in short, romantic love is only one element of love, and not its foundation.

No, the love I had for my wife would be there no matter what she did. That doesn't mean, however, that I would do whatever she wanted. It didn't mean I would allow her to cheat on me and continue without any consequences, up to and if necessary, divorce. But even if I had gone through and divorced her, I would still love her and want what was best for her. To me, if love isn't that solid, it isn't real marital love. If you marry only for what your spouse can do for you, how he or she makes you feel, then that is not love. It is only a shadow of love with no foundation for the fullness of love.

So the fact my wife had cheated on me didn't mean that love withered away on the vine. No matter how much she might hurt me, my love for her wouldn't change. If we had to separate and/or divorce, I would ache for the loss and love her still, even if we could no longer stay married due to continued infidelity.

So when my priest asked me that question, I quickly said no. I was more concerned for the fact that she was spiritually lost, and hoped I could save her with God's help, than I was on the fact she'd hurt me and stolen from me. I feared for her soul. If there was an opportunity to save her and our marriage, I wanted to give that a chance. I couldn't see after 29 years just giving up and walking away without a fight.

So I told my priest my plan to confront her. I had given it plenty of thought the night before, and decided I would keep it under raps until we arrived at our anniversary location. My priest didn't think the plan would work, but he did warn me that we could get there, I could confront her, and she may not want to continue and wish to return home. She may want out of the marriage herself.

Even though I knew that was possible, I hadn't seriously thought about it. It would make for a very tense ride back home if that happened. So our conversation ended after he encouraged me.

The problem was our anniversary was three days away now. That meant I had to keep this heart-rending knowledge that I knew her secret quiet for three days, and the whole 2-3 hour trip to the bed and breakfast as well. I knew that was going to be a tall order. It would be hard for me to hide that. Plus, she was still in "wanting to have sex at every available opportunity" mode, and I had no idea how to handle that. Could I really pretend that everything was okay to do that? I had my doubts. As it turned out, I didn't have to wait long.

That day, I headed out on lunch break. I usually came home for lunch. It just so happened that she was going home at the same time as she had an hour or so before going to her next client. She called me up and asked me if I wanted to have sex when I got home. I said yes, and we hung up. But I realized then, I couldn't go through with it. I couldn't go home and act like everything was fine. I would have to confront her then.

When I walked in the door, she was at the computer. She quickly shut it down and said hi. But when she turned around, she could immediately see I was distressed. Her smile turned into concern, and she asked, "What's wrong?"

I sat in a chair in the middle of the living room, and she sat on my lap facing me. I stared her in the eyes and asked point blank, "Are you cheating on me?"

She paused for a moment and said, "Not really."

I had asked her that, hoping she would come clean with everything. The one advantage to having read her confession is I knew most everything she'd done, even the worst of it. So I would know if she was holding anything back from me. This obviously wasn't jumping right in with a full confession and that saddened me, but the "not really" certainly meant, "yes." Any hope I had at that point that it was just pretend for sex chatting purposes vanished with those words and the way she'd said them.

So I gave her another chance to confess. I then said, "What if I told you I know you have been?"

She sighed, and I waited. Then she said, "Guess I should tell you everything."

I said, "That would be a good place to start."

She then proceeded to tell me the details about her online activity and Bubba in as much detail as I could expect. Yet she didn't mention anything about Clyde. So I asked her, "What about Clyde?" She nodded and divulged all that I knew about her experience with Clyde, including things I didn't know like the week he returned and how she barely escaped having intercourse with him.

On the one hand, I was heartbroken to know it was all true. Part of me still held out that it was a mistake or misunderstanding, or that she knew I was using a key logger and faked the whole thing to teach me a lesson. But she didn't know I had learned of it from the computer. She thought most likely either I had seen them together or a friend of mine had and told me.

But I was relieved that she told me everything. One of the reasons I waited until she had done so before divulging how I found out. I wanted to know she was being honest with me, and thankfully she was.

As I've learned being on a support group for spouses who have gone through affairs, the unfaithful partners, once caught, tend to not tell anymore than they think they have to. This results in what is called the "trickle truth." The spouse learns of some truth, but not all. They go through the trauma of the experience. Then a few months or weeks down the road, more comes out and they start back at square one again. Then another period of time passes and yet more comes out. By that time, any attempt at rebuilding trust becomes near impossible, as the hurt spouses never knows if they have the whole story, never knows if their spouse is being completely honest with them. With each new revelation that the unfaithful spouse has been lying, the trust meter sinks lower and lower into the negative.

The only way true rebuilding can happen is to get all the cards out on the table at once, so that there won't be anymore "gotchas" in the rebuilding process. Because to me, trust is key in an intimate relationship. Without it, you don't have a functioning marriage. If I can't trust her to be committed to me and me only on the martial front, then our ability to have an intimate relationship is significantly damaged, and we might as well separate, no matter how much we love one another.

So once we'd talked through all the details and her confession, and she had confessed to everything I knew she'd done as I learned from her chat log, I had one more question to ask. It was an answer I feared the most, because her reaction would determine whether we rebuilt our marriage or went our separate ways.

I asked her, "Do you want me or him?"

Her response was immediate. She said, "You, you, you, you!" She wrapped her arms around me in a big hug. I let out a big breath and relaxed. I had feared either she would say, "Him," or she'd be ambivalent and say, "I don't know." Unfortunately, many unfaithful spouses can't make up their mind. When caught, they aren't ready to give up the affair partner, but they don't want to lose their marriage. Fortunately for me, from that moment, she made it clear that she would sacrifice everyone to stay with me. That was what I wanted to hear most of all: a level of commitment that would make rebuilding successfully a possibility.

I then told her what needed to happen. She needed to break it totally off with Bubba, and once done, never contact him again. She agreed. That agreement would be tested in the weeks to come. As she discovered, when you've really come to love someone that intimately, stopping cold turkey is not for the faint of heart. Yet I made it clear that was what had to happen and she acknowledged that fact.

I also made it clear that the success of rebuilding was mostly in her hands. I would do what I could, but she would have to rebuild my trust in her, and that would take a while. She would have to discover why she allowed herself to fall into that trap and take measures to never let it happen again. She would have a lot of spiritual work to do as well. I knew our priest would see to that.

But I had hope. Her confessing the whole affair left me feeling I did have the whole story, that she was being honest with me. I could tell she was ready to dump it all and stay with me, and that was encouraging. I didn't understand how she could have done what she did at that point. In truth, still don't totally *understand* it even though I understand the *how* of what happened. But for me, I was more concerned that she not do it again than I was that she'd done it. If I could be assured it wouldn't happen again, then I could heal. If not, then there was little hope.

This assurance was confirmed in another way that evening. As we were going to bed, she asked if I was able to have sex with her again. I had been giving that some thought and wasn't sure how to approach it, or how to determine if and when I could. I wanted to for several reasons. One, her last sexual experience was with Bubba, and I didn't want that to be the last one she'd had for however long it took me to arrive at being ready. I feared it would create a longing for him. Two, in her state of wanting sex as often as possible, withholding it might make it that much harder for her to focus on rebuilding and provide more temptation to return to Bubba for a fix. Three, there was a sense of wanting to reclaim what was mine, since I wasn't the last one to have sex with her.

But I didn't want to convey the message that everything was okay and normal either. She'd hurt me in a big way. How could I engage in that activity in less than 24 hours of discovering she'd been cheating on me? When she asked that question, I didn't have a good answer. But as I thought about it, one came to me.

I conveyed my understanding of what sex means in a marriage, that it is a martial sacrament that bonds two people into one flesh. That she had violated that by bonding herself to another man. I made it clear that I cannot stand for her to bond with anyone other than me in that way. If she had sex with me, it would be her committing to me to never bond with another in that way again. To break that sacred promise was to tell me I can't trust her.

The truth was, I couldn't trust her at that point. So I came up with another concept. After all, I knew if rebuilding was going to work, there was a certain level of trust that had to be given. But it wasn't there at that point. It would take months to rebuild that trust.

So what did I do? I told her that by doing this, I was giving her trust on loan. She would be paying that back in the months ahead by proving to me that I could really trust her again. But because I knew for rebuilding to work, I would have to trust her on some level, I told her I was loaning her trust. If she defaulted, then I'd have to repossess the marital agreement, and she would have to "pay as you go" instead.

This accomplished some important steps. One, she knew her future performance was key in whether we rebuilt trust successfully. Two, it was in her hands. She was paying me back by rebuilding trust. To fail to do that, she knew would result in a much more difficult situation if she violated it. Three, it provided a framework that gave the best chance for her to succeed in rebuilding. It established a way to have some continued support from me, while not giving the appearance as if I had no problems with what she'd done.

I asked her if she was ready to commit to that by having sex with me. She said she was, and we did. The good news is, to date, she has paid back that trust loan and never defaulted. However, it had a shaky start.

So ended the first day after I discovered the truth on May 11, 2011. The confrontation had turned out about as good as I could have hoped, short of finding out it wasn't all true. But I knew we had a long road ahead of us, and I didn't know what it would hold or if we'd make it. For the first time in our marriage, reaching our next anniversary was in question. I honestly didn't know how this would come out.

The Path to Rebuilding

When a couple who have gone through infidelity decide to stay together, it is called rebuilding. Not remodeling. Unfortunately, in too many cases, one or both of the spouses tend to treat it as remodeling, if even that. Remodeling would be to make a change here or there, add to the marriage, tweak the relationship. Ultimately, the goal is to get back to "normal." That is, the goal is to return to how the relationship was before the affair. The affair is treated as something to get past rather than something that changes everything about the relationship.

It is a rebuilding because what the couple has experienced is a loss. A very deep loss, especially for the hurt spouse, but also for the unfaithful spouse once they face the reality of what they've done. A loss that means what existed before the affair is destroyed, gone, dead. Especially when adultery is involved in an affair, the marriage itself has been significantly damaged. There is a sense in which the act of sexual intercourse bonds a person to another, and in so doing, violates the bond previously established. A person literally marries everyone they have sexual intercourse with on at least a physical level. More on that in part 4. But the bottom line is the marriage has been lost. What a couple had prior to an affair will not and should not return to being "normal."

In essence, it is like a house that is destroyed during a storm. You don't remodel it. You clear the debris and rebuild the building into something new or you decide to build in a new location. When this happens, there are two realities to keep in mind.

One, because the affair is a significant loss, most people will go through the stages of grief: denial, anger, bargaining, depression, and acceptance. One chapter in Part 4 goes through those, but here we note that it will come. You will tend to experience most, if not all these emotions. Only when you come to acceptance can a person move forward into healing. Everyone has a different timeline on how fast they move through them. Some take a few months, others can take years.

Two, instituting these changes on such a massive scale will result in a big identity change for both individuals and their relationship. What that means is it will take a minimum of two years, if all goes well, for the new identity to feel like part of who you are instead of something tacked onto you. For some months, you will feel "this isn't me," and wish a return to how it used to be—even if the changes are good and positive.

For me, it took around nine months to a year to emerge from feeling like the changes we made were "not me." Now, more than a year and a half as I write this, the changes feel normal, natural, and how it should be. In my case, I healed faster than most. Part of that was my personality. A big part of it, however, was how well Lenita did in the rebuilding. If she had not done what she should have, I would still be suffering. I've seen people in our support group in that situation, and it is almost always a result of sweeping issues under the rug and not dealing with them, usually by the unfaithful spouse, but sometimes also by the hurt spouse.

In parts 2 through 4 of this book, we will offer a series of articles that we pray will be used as support for the couple going through rebuilding, as well as some issues concerning infidelity in general. But in the last chapters of part 1, I wanted to give a topical outline of what we did that helped us heal so fast. Again, not all this will apply to everyone. Some things are particular to us. But there are some general principles you'll see emerge, and I pray, some encouragement as to what a successful rebuilding looks like.

The Emotional Roller Coaster Ride

Four days after discovery day, we headed out for our 29th wedding anniversary. It was and, I pray, will always be the most unusual anniversary we've ever had. In terms of dealing with the affairs, however, it gave us one huge benefit. We were able to spend almost three days separated from our daily lives and focus intensely on each other. We hashed out the implications of what had happened and planned for the future, giving our rebuilding a strong launch. We had a good time, but more importantly, we talked constantly about what had happened and what needed to happen if we were to make it. We laid an important foundation during those days that helped us not only to reconnect but to hope.

Then we returned home to our daily lives. Now would be the time for her to follow-through on her promises and commitments. Would she succeed? Would we make it or run our marital ship aground as we attempted to rebuild? The possible paths rebuilding could take seemed endless—divorce the outcome for most of them. While I'd gained some hope during our anniversary get-away, I knew success hung by a thin thread. In the initial days after our trip, that thread appeared to be snapping.

Historically, I'm a very emotionally subdued person. I've always been that way. When my son threw a stick and broke our window, I didn't get mad. I didn't blow up. I didn't yell at him about how stupid that was. That scenario has played out multiple times. I simply don't get angry. At least, very easily.

Likewise, I was on my high school tennis team for three years. One of the guys dubbed me, "Mr. Spock" because when I blew a point, I didn't give any hint of emotional response like he did, usually banging his racket on the ground or on the net post.

In some cases, it means I don't get angry and emotionally motivated about something when I should. Even Jesus knew when to get angry about something. But in other cases, it has been a blessing. In the case of Lenita's affair, it was a blessing.

That said, you wouldn't know I was a low emotional person the first three weeks after discovery day. Once we returned from our anniversary trip, I was up and down. I was so emotionally distraught that I felt shortness of breath. I had images of me having a heart attack merely from the adrenaline pumping through my system. I'd never experienced that before.

One day in particular, I was on my way to work, and the fear that she was heading back to his house that morning was overwhelming. By the time I got to work, I couldn't think about anything else. I stared at the screen, and tears kept wanting to spill out. I would heave trying to keep myself from bursting out in a giant bawl right there in the office. After an hour of trying to keep my composure, I realized it was a losing situation, and I decided to make it a sick day because, boy was I sick. I headed back home. I heard one of my coworkers say as I passed her office, "What's wrong with Rick?"

For a good month to two months, all I could think about every minute of the day was the affair. I would sit at work and try to get something done, only to find myself staring at the monitor, lost in thoughts about the affair. I had to literally force myself to do any work. About all that I did during that time was what absolutely had to be done or my job would all come crashing in. Otherwise, I stared at the computer screen, lost in the various thoughts about what had happened, trying to figure out what would happen.

After that period of time, it started getting better for me. In part because, like I said, I'm not that emotional of person. So I could only stay in that state for so long. But also because by four weeks out, I began to feel like the affair was really over. It allowed me to relax and the emotions of fear to gradually die off. After four weeks, the emotions became more manageable. Others take much longer. I still thought a lot about it, and my world was still shaky, but I could see then it was headed in the right directions. But those first four weeks? They were the most emotionally crazy time in my life I had ever experienced.

No Contact

If there was one area that Lenita stumbled on in the early days of rebuilding, it was no contact. This is not uncommon, and in truth, she did better than most unfaithful spouses do. But it was one of the reasons for my emotional state during those first four weeks. I didn't have an assurance that the affair was over until I knew she'd broken all contact with Bubba and any other affair partners online.

Concerning the main online site she'd been having sex chats on, she agreed early on to shut it down. I stood over her shoulder and watched as she deleted her account. It was a while later until she deleted her MySpace account that had started her online activity, but I knew she didn't go there any longer and I had her log in and could check to make sure that was true.

In all, she promised three times that, "This is the last contact with him," that is, Bubba. First time she said those words was on our anniversary. She had told him it was over. They'd said their goodbys. She had promised me no more contact with Bubba. As far as her contacting him, she kept that with one exception. Her problem was anytime he contacted her, she felt like she had to respond. He kept texting her on her phone, and she kept responding to him.

I attempted to tell her that she shouldn't respond to him. No contact meant no contact, period. But she felt like a lot of unfaithful spouses do about their affair partners, especially if it was ongoing when caught. Admittedly, breaking off a relationship in which you loved someone is a hard thing to do. Even if you know the relationship is wrong. Lenita felt responsible for the pain he was experiencing, and continued to feel like she needed to help him. At one point, she told me that she needed to break contact gradually. She couldn't do it cold turkey.

But she fell into the trap most unfaithful spouses fall into. The mind really is not ready to let go of the affair partner, so they find any excuse to keep the door open. Looking back on it, she realizes several things. One, gradually would have never closed the door all the way on her affair partner. She would always feel like she needed to help him. She did for almost nine months. Two, you never get closure. A lot of unfaithful partners feel a need for closure. Any who initiated contact for that reason report it didn't help, it made it worse. As Lenita says now, what more closure did she need? She'd told him it was over, said her goodbyes, what more was there to say?

The first two weeks were the worse. He would text her. She'd respond. Sometimes with a message that she hoped he would be okay, but she had to focus on her marriage and that she wouldn't be contacting him again. Only to have him text again, and her respond again.

The first Thursday after we returned from our anniversary was the worst. She was still arguing that she had to cut him off her way, which meant slowly, which for me was emotional "water torture." I even told her how it was all affecting me, why she needed to cut it off and not respond to him. All to no avail.

That evening, I was stressing out about what to do. She was telling me when he texted and what he said, but she was being very vague about what she wrote back to him. I decided I needed to find out. So once she fell asleep, I opened her phone text and began reading. I found one interaction she'd told me about, and read her responses. One jumped out at me, and sent me into stress overload as if the whole affair had reignited.

She had told Bubba that they couldn't communicate over text or phone. But if he ever saw her car in a parking lot, he could turn the magnetic sign on her door upside down so she'd know he'd been there. Granted, it was very minor, but for me symbolized that it wasn't over. She didn't tell me about this secret sign between them, and she initiated a form of communication with him.

When she saw me that Friday morning, she saw I was stressed about something. I confronted her with what I'd found on her phone. She acknowledged that it was wrong, but she felt bad for him. She also was peeved that I looked on her phone without asking her to show me. That was all well and good, but I didn't trust that she'd tell me if she kept secrets still. Finding that text confirmed my fears.

Over the second week, the attitude continued. Bubba would text her and she would respond. By the Thursday of that week, I'd stood over her shoulder as she made one "final" text to Bubba in response to another of his text, telling him this was it, she wouldn't be responding to anymore of his text. It sounded strong enough. She let me read it before she sent it. I approved and she sent it.

But as she fell asleep and I sat at my desk, I felt she'd probably respond if he texted again. [illegible] n no ability to not respond to him. With the stress I wa[illegible] om the continued contact, she might stop telling me about th[illegible] she thought it was going to make me worse.

So I decided I would do something to ensure she kept her word this time. So I logged onto our online cell phone account and added a parental control service to her phone number. That allowed me to go in and add numbers to block from ever showing up on her phone, both calls and texts. Then I added Bubba's number to the block list. Once done, I deleted all evidence of it from her emails (all admin emails went to her email address).

Over the weekend, I felt much, much better. She was happier, thinking Bubba had given it up and moved on. But as we were headed to my second—her third—marital counseling session on Monday, I felt a little guilty as well. I had decided to talk with the counselor about it and she confirmed what I thought. I wanted Lenita to be transparent with me, but I was hiding something from her.

But I wanted to wait until we sat before the counselor to tell her, so the counselor could help us deal with it. So after I talked with the counselor in private, we brought Lenita back in and I told her what I'd done.

She was angry, but didn't show it much in the session. It came out during our drive home. She hated two things about it other than the fact I had gone behind her back. One, she had thought Bubba was doing better, and had stopped calling her on his own. That made her feel better about him, like he was moving on. Now she found out he likely still had tried and was probably not okay.

Two, she felt I had forced her to respond in a way she didn't want to. She didn't feel right about simply not responding, feeling that would be hateful. Of course, that is exactly what needed to happen, and that only served to confirm to me that she wouldn't have stopped responding to his text. That her promise of, "I'll not respond to anything else" was nothing more than hot air for my sake.

So on the way back I asked her if she wanted me to take the block off. She still sounded angry, but said no. It did serve one purpose, because she feared when she got a text that it would be him. With the block on, she didn't have to worry that she'd hurt me more by responding. Even though she didn't like what I'd done, she accepted it, and one and a half years later the block is still in place. Not so much for my peace of mind, but because she likes knowing she isn't likely to see a text from h[illegible]ough I'm sure he gave up a long time ago.

After that, I began to feel lik[illegible] affair had truly ended. It took another week or two for it to sink in that he was no longer contacting her, and she didn't have anymore contact with him, that I could tell, but for me, that's when the affair ended, when Bubba stopped texting her because I blocked his number.

There were, however, a couple of dying gasps. In June, he started following her in his car. Maybe hoping she'd see him and pull over. One of her clients lived on his block, and so when he drove by while she was there, he would creep by. She tended to look out the bathroom window that faced that street and see him sometimes.

At one point that month, he left a note on her car, asking her to come to his house to visit. She, feeling a need to respond, wrote a similar note saying she couldn't do that and was focused on her marriage. Then she placed it on his car, came home, and told me about the incident.

At that point, I felt like if I didn't do something, he was going to keep attempting to make contact with her. I didn't want her to once again contact and tell him, "No, this is it." One, I didn't want her to break no contact to tell him that. So far that had not worked. Two, that's what he wanted, any contact with her. I didn't want to give that to him on a silver platter. Three, she said he feared me. He had an irrational fear that I could get on his computer and install a virus or something. He wasn't very smart about technology, and Lenita had painted me as a computer whiz.

So I decided I would write an email to him, in a nice way, telling him to back off. I figured if he knew she was telling me everything, even about the note he'd left her, he'd likely stop. So I noted that she'd told me about him following her, driving slowly by the house, about the note, etc. In my best way, told him it was over, he needed to accept that and leave her alone. I wrote it, Lenita reviewed it and suggested changes, then I let her press the send button.

He sent an email back within the hour, agreeing to not try and contact her anymore. Though some of his wording minimized what had happened, I felt I had accomplished my purpose. If he lived up to his word, that would be the end of it.

That held for about two months. During August, Lenita changed the day of the week she cleaned that particular house in Bubba's neighborhood. For some reason, this triggered him to start doing the same things. He'd follow her, drive by the house slowly, all those types of activities to force an "accidental" meeting between them in the hopes they would fire it all back up.

So again I sent another email. This time I threatened to obtain a restraining order. I also made the point that if she wanted to, she could have easily gone to his house without my knowledge. The fact she hadn't done that should tell him something.

I could say that with confidence because the one positive affect his attempts to contact her had on me is it confirmed she'd been telling me the truth about not having any contact with him. If she had been, she wouldn't tell me about contacts with him. If she had been, he certainly wouldn't be stalking her. The fact he stalked her gave me confidence that she had kept her word and there was no contact with him.

After that email, he again responded and said again that he acknowledged that he shouldn't be doing these things and that it was over, he'd not seek her out again. After that email, to date, he has kept his word.

But there is another aspect to the no contact than direct contact. It involves objects of remembrances. Lenita had several of these. Some I knew about, like her pictures of Clyde and Bubba. She kept them in a folder on her computer and phone, but didn't go look at them very much. She also had some papers in her purse that were either things they'd given her or the address of Clyde she'd looked up on the Internet.

I had told her she needed to get rid of these as they would only get in the way of allowing their memories to die as much as possible. Yet, I refrained from forcing her to get rid of them. She said she wasn't ready. She still hung in the fog to a degree and was attached to them, and these items were all she had left of them. So I decided to use the items as evidence she was progressing. I knew if she was healing and getting past it, at some point she'd get rid of these things.

It took about five or six months, but it happened. One day, she announced she was ready to get rid of the stuff. She cleaned her phone, her computer, and purse of all items. She even went into folders on her computer that I didn't know about. Emails, MySpace account, Facebook messages, all deleted. When that happened, I felt she'd taken a major step. She had detached herself fully from the affair partners. It represented the last evidence that no contact had been fully implemented and the affairs were behind us.

If anything, the trouble we had with her going no contact illustrates a key reality of rebuilding. The trouble she had was, in the bigger scheme of things, not nearly as big a deal as what many hurt spouses get from their unfaithful spouse. Often rebuilding is the old, "one step forward, two steps back" feeling. Even in the best of rebuilding experiences, don't expect it to run perfectly smooth.

Transparency

The two biggest and immediate keys to rebuilding is no contact with the affair partner and transparency. In truth, transparency is a key characteristic of a healthy marriage, whether an affair has happened or not. What one spouse does affects the other. Hidden secrets especially. While I'm not saying you have to divulge your journal you've kept since a kid, marriage is about intimacy. The only way to be intimate is to be open and transparent. Any secret you don't want the spouse to know about is an area of your life he is not intimate with you in and weakens the marriage.

Especially once a spouse has had an affair, the need to rebuild trust demands total transparency. What does this mean, practically?

For my wife, she gave me full access to her cell phone, email accounts, Facebook account, MySpace account, the online social forum where she did most of her sex chatting (that was closed down pretty early). If I asked for access to anything, she gave it to me.

But the bigger aspect of transparency often overlooked by many is honestly answering all questions and being willing to talk and hash through it all with me. Way too often I hear from other hurt spouses, "My spouse won't talk about it." Or after two or three months of discussing it, some will say, "That's it. I'm done talking about it. We just need to move on."

What this does is prevent the hurt spouse from healing. It blocks transparency. Thankfully, if there was any one area where Lenita excelled in the rebuilding from day one, it was in always being willing to discuss what happened in the affairs, no matter how much it hurt her to do so. I attribute a large part of our success in rebuilding to that fact. Even more than two years after I had discovered her affairs, I knew I could ask any question I wanted about them and she would answer it. I knew she would give me an honest answer.

From the second question I asked her on discovery day, she has always told me everything, save the one item in the first week I mentioned in no contact. That has been her sole slip up.

However, I had secrets. If she was going to be transparent, I need to as well. My secrets weren't as big as hers, by any means, but I had them. On our anniversary I divulged everything I could think of. I wanted her to know I was in this with her. Because a healthy marriage is transparent.

A quick example of something I shared. I had a boss who was a woman. We often ate lunches together because it was convenient and no one likes to eat alone. We mostly focused on business and occasionally would talk about our kids. But that was as far as it ever went. Nothing went on between us beyond a business relationship. There never was, to put it in many unfaithful spouse's terms, any "chemistry" between us. We were friends. Lenita knew about these frequent lunches. But she trusted me, and I didn't think anything about them myself because I knew they were just lunches with the boss type thing.

My boss was released by our employer. She wanted to keep the friendship alive. One time we agreed to meet for lunch. I went, but didn't tell Lenita. I admit, I felt a little more uncomfortable because now it wasn't business. Not that anything would happen or did I expect it to. Yet, I feared that someone might see me eating with another woman who knew us and it would get back to Lenita and look bad. So I decided to avoid a one-on-one eating situation in the future, just to keep boundaries clear. Of if we did, to let Lenita know about it.

So that was one of the things I confessed. At the time, it didn't seem like any big deal. But in light of Lenita's affair, it took on a whole different flavor. It looked like something someone would do who was having an affair. It was a boundary I crossed that could have gone wrong if circumstances had been favorable to it. But in the interest of being transparent with her, I told her about the lunch date I had with my former boss. Who, by the way, is still a good friend.

Transparency and no contact with the affair partners are two of the key events that need to happen if rebuilding is to succeed. Lenita, once she got past those texts with Bubba, has done an outstanding job of no contact. I've never had the evidence or impression that she has tried to initiate contact with him herself. On transparency, Lenita has put most unfaithful spouses to shame. Her attitude has always been, "I asked for this, you didn't." So no matter how much it hurt her to talk about something, she did it without blaming me for anything, without minimizing what she did (save when her own mind didn't remember it right), or not being willing to face the guilt and pain of what she did, even to date.

Falling Out of Love

One of the harder things for unfaithful spouses to do once their affair has been discovered, if they felt any love or attraction to their affair partner, is to stop loving them. It is equally hard for the hurt spouse to know that their spouse has such feelings for another person.

Lenita had two kinds of attractions to get over. One attraction was with Clyde. Born out of an irrational, addictive infatuation with his attention, by discovery day she still had a strong attachment to him despite having not seen him in about five months. Yet, she had other online sex-chat partners and her affair partner that occupied her mind and attention. It's not that she cared for Clyde as a person so much (she knew he didn't care about her), but she was infatuated with the exciting feelings his attention gave her. She kept his picture on her phone to look at occasionally but thought about him daily.

However, the relationship she had with Bubba was more of a real love. He became the daily companion I wasn't. She spent lots of time with him either in person or via different forms of messaging. In the six weeks of their affair, she said they had sex about twice a week. Sex, for her, just came with the package. At first, she wasn't that attracted to him, but he grew on her. By the time I discovered the affair, she had convinced herself that she could love two men successfully, and had admitted to herself that she loved Bubba as well as me.

These men occupied her thoughts daily by discovery day. Though my discovering her affairs shook her out of her fog-thinking a good bit, one can't so easily turn off how one feels about someone. She had fallen in love with another man. While after the first three weeks she successfully didn't have direct contact with him, she kept mementos of him up until five or six months after discovery day. When she gave those up, I knew we were making progress.

Still, both men, Bubba more so, remained in her thoughts daily. Early on, she learned about the art of guarding one's thoughts. Our priest helped with that, by suggesting she wear a rubber band around her wrist, and when she realized she was dwelling on any of the men in the affairs, or about the affairs themselves in any kind of positive light, she would snap the rubber band to remind her not to think about them.

It took nearly a full year of no contact and guarding her thoughts before she realized one day, "I don't care about them like I used to." She no longer felt "in love" with either of them. But it took time and work to arrive there.

Many will think just time alone will do the trick, and it can if no contact is maintained. Eventually after a few years, you'll find you aren't thinking about them so much. But that doesn't mean you're no longer are in love with them. When you think about them, you can still feel the excitement of the relationship. Then if the opportunity to connect with them presents itself again, it can easily flare back into a roaring fire. To avoid that scenario, you have to no longer care about them and view the affairs as one big disaster with no redeeming qualities.

In essence, what Lenita did was to go extreme no contact, even in her thoughts about them. Thoughts of them would pop up regularly, but she'd trained herself not to dwell on them. They would pass through.

One day not long before writing this, almost one and a half years after discovery day, she realized that she didn't think one time about Bubba the previous day. We had attended our son's band day at college, and her mind was all wrapped up in that and our day together. Yes, it took nearly one and a half years of doing what needed to be done before she had her first day when not one thought of him popped into her head. As I've told her before, in five years, you'll think about him even less. Ten years, he probably won't even be on your radar but once to twice during the year, if that.

Then a few days later, she actually became angry at Clyde for having manipulated her with his fantasies. It was the first time she saw what I had always seen: she'd been duped with a pack of lies. He'd sold her for the only thing he cared about, sex. It didn't matter to him that he was causing a husband years of pain, or potentially destroying a marriage and family for his little conquest. For the first time she became angry at him as I had been since discovery day.

But this is the progress when someone is doing all they can to fall out of love. Too many unfaithful spouses don't do that. There remains for years a feeling of love and excitement about the affair, even while they tell their spouse they love them and will remain faithful. If left to grow and stay, the likelihood of a future entanglement remains high. Additionally, it can effect the relationship with your spouse because part of your heart is still with the affair partner(s). Your spouse doesn't have all of you. Letting the love for the affair partner die is hard work, and agonizing at first. But if the rebuilding is to succeed, it has to happen so you can return that part of your heart to your spouse.

Getting Help

Shortly after discovery day, we sought help to work through our crisis. A lot of people don't and flounder because of it. Let's face it, for most people who go through this, it is their first time. Yes, some face it multiple times, but all the more reason to seek help because what had been done before obviously didn't work as it should have. But all of us who experience infidelity do so for the first time at some point. Few have enough information or an idea of what steps are needed to heal the situation or decide whether healing together is going to work or not.

As the hurt spouse, I decided on discovery day that we likely had one chance to get this right. If she went back into it, I didn't think I could handle it. But if our marriage was to end over this, I wanted to go into it saying I'd done all I could to save it. I'd given every reasonable opportunity for her to fix the problem. Therefore I didn't want to leave one stone unturned. I knew I didn't know enough of what to do, so we sought help. Thankfully, she had the same attitude I did.

On our way to our 29th anniversary getaway, we read our first book. Lenita felt the affair had swept her into a whirlpool that she couldn't escape. The addictive nature of what she felt and how she thought during the affair caused her to conclude she must be a sex addict. To that end, we bought our first book, *Healing the Wounds of Sexual Addiction* by Mark Lasser. The book had a lot of good points, but some of it seemed extreme for our situation when it came to what to do. But as we found out later, that is because experiencing an addiction for a period of time doesn't make one an addict.

We discovered this when we started counseling. Up to this point, I'd never been to a counselor for anything. I'd never felt like I needed one, though there were times I really should have found one for our marriage. Lenita was eager to get help to save our marriage. She sought out and found a marriage counselor. The week following our anniversary trip, she went for her first visit alone. Monday of the following week we went together and continued seeing the counselor weekly until mid-July. It ended earlier than it probably should have, but we'd made good progress by that point. It ended mainly because I was losing my job and we didn't know what our financial situation was going to be like.

In Lenita's first session with her, the counselor ruled out her being a sex addict. The reason is that a sex addict has a long history of addictive behaviors. There are usually markers during childhood, family life, teen years, patterns of being sexually abused, and problems controlling one's self in many areas including sexual behaviors. Lenita, by contrast, had never acted like she was addicted to these things at all. For 28.5 years, she hardly cared about sex very much. Seven months of experiencing an addiction to a feeling doesn't make one a sex addict.

But our counselor, in ruling out her being a sex addict, saw what she felt was the real problem. As discussed in the pre-affair breakdown of our marriage, it became apparent that what attracted Lenita to these men was what I wasn't giving her: attention, time, and making her feel I loved her. For 29 years, we'd taken each other for granted. We'd become "comfortable" in living with the dysfunctional aspects of our relationship.

It is much like what happened at the college I attended back in the 1980s. One day in chapel, they displayed a slideshow of all the trashy spots on campus that would look bad to a first time visitor. Junk lying around, a dirt pathway cutting across the grassy mall area, chipping paint or broken areas. Everyone was stunned. We'd become so used to the blemishes, we didn't notice them. For the first time since I had attended that college, when the students exited chapel they walked on the sidewalk around the grass instead of across the mall.

To that end, our counselor had us stop reading the book on sexual addiction, and pointed us to a book called *His Needs, Her Needs* by Willard F. Jr. Harley. More on that book later. But to put it briefly, it was exactly the book we needed at that time. It opened both our eyes to what we'd done to each other throughout our marriage, and why although we felt we loved one another very much, we'd lost the passionate feeling of love for one another, leaving us more vulnerable to the temptation of infidelity.

After that book, we read another highly recommended to us by our online support group, called *Not Just Friends*, by Shirley Glass. It opened our eyes to what had gone wrong during the affair, and Lenita discovered what happened to her isn't all that unique. We continued to read books and still do to this day. We usually read them in the car when we're by ourselves going to church or any other outing. To date we've read through seven books. Some of them not dealing with affairs, but marriage in general.

One other type of help we sought out was an online support group. I had two reasons for doing that. The obvious was a support group would be a good way to help us not feel alone in the struggle, and a good place for advice. I also wanted it to be online. Both for anonymity, but also because I'd had Lenita shut down her account where she sex chatted a lot. I wanted that void to be filled with a new group of people who would be supportive of her rebuilding.

I did some searching, and found an online site called "Daily Strength." It had a plethora of support groups from weight loss, exercise, healthy eating, divorce, sexual addictions, other types of addictions, and of course, one forum called "Infidelity." Upon checking it out, it seemed perfect. Not only did it provide an active group of people going through the same things we were, but a place to journal, which I thought would be a good thing for me especially. I needed to get this out of my system by writing. If I can put it on "paper," I can process it.

That group has been a godsend for many reasons. We've made some good friends there. For me personally, it provided some purpose to going through my affair. I'm one that learns quickly and reaffirms that by helping others to learn it as well. I found that I had a new ministry. It gave some redemption to the situation to know it would enable me to help others get through this ordeal. Through doing that, I learned more and it helped me process what I dealt with.

By now we're "old hands" there. We've seen a wide variety of situations on both sides of the fence parade through. Like many there, we help where we can. The articles in the next parts of this book were written from our experiences there. The group has been a wealth of information and support.

Lenita, despite being the "cheating spouse," has gained a large measure of respect by both hurt spouses and unfaithful spouses through her success in rebuilding and working on herself, as well as her advice to various people since being there. Most hurt spouses there wish they had an unfaithful spouse as dedicated to healing herself, her marriage, and me as Lenita has been.

Seeking help is a given if you want to rebuild. To not do so is the same thing when a storm destroys your house and you need to rebuild it. Do you grab a hammer and hope you can figure out how to put it back together? Or do you call a contractor, plumber, electrician, etc.? Only if you are an expert in all those areas at once would you think about attempting it, and even then you'd be nuts. No different with a marriage that has gone downhill into an affair. It takes someone with experience and objectivity to see the path out of the swamp. Someone who knows the way. It is not embarrassing to ask for directions when you are really lost. It is necessary.

Spiritual Revival

As stated earlier, we are both Christians. Statistics show that percentage wise, Christians have as high a rate of infidelity as non-Christians. However, that's including all who make a claim of being Christian, but don't regularly go to church or have a vibrant spiritual life. When one weeds out the uncommitted Christians, the divorce rate and therefore the related infidelity rate drops. Yet, they are not zero.

Most people would have classified us as committed Christians. We both attended church every Sunday unless prevented. We both had daily prayer lives. We weren't perfect. There is always room for improvement. Likely the fact that I considered Lenita to be often a better Christian than myself, led me to find it highly unlikely she would ever be unfaithful to me.

With her weight loss, her interest in her new body, and the attention she received from it, she concurrently began to focus less on God and spiritual matters. While she still attended church services on Sunday, because the whole family went, these became less important to her and she rarely wanted to attend any additional services.

By the time Clyde came along, God had a weakened place in her heart. As Clyde showed her attention, and internally she knew what she was doing was wrong, God was tucked away inside a closet so she didn't have to think about how He viewed what she did. The deeper she went into the quicksand, the more God was shoved to the side so He wouldn't interfere.

As Clyde ate away at her morals, and the online sex chats deadened her conscious to the values she'd always held so dear in her life, she more easily gave into the passions within her. Whereas at first she fought against the desire to give into Clyde's wishes, by the time Bubba came along, she gave in without barely a whimper.

The last thing she wanted to do was to face God. As the affair with Clyde deepened, she stopped praying altogether. Our priest noticed that she seemed to be "checked out" of the services. He figured she was tired all the time. But really, the services were a weekly reminder that God was still there, and she didn't want to think about Him or the life He had called her to. She only wanted to fulfill her passions.

During the affair, there were two key things that happened in relation to her affair and God. One was the deception. Usually before the Easter service, we are expected to go to confession. We tend to do this as a family, so it wasn't easy for her to skip this. It would have been noticed and raised suspicions. That was the last thing she wanted to do. By this point she was deep into the affair with Bubba and having sex with him.

Usually our priest asks a series of questions, like a doctor might in diagnosing a sickness. One of those questions always is, "Are you involved in any inappropriate relationships?" She answered, no, lying to God and the priest, and hiding her sin. During the whole time of the affairs, she readily partook of the Eucharist, which for someone in her situation is dangerous. So she did her best to put on a front that everything was fine spiritually when it wasn't.

As mentioned earlier, she also had these moments of clarity where she would pray to God, usually at church, to save her from herself. She knew she was on a downward spiral, that she was hurting me and the kids. But she felt trapped. Other than those brief prayers, she hid from God and kept Him at arms length. For all practical purposes, she'd become totally a Christian in name only, playing the part.

So it is no surprise that after discovery day, one of her primary areas of healing involved her spiritual healing. For nearly a full year, she went to confession weekly. These were invaluable to her, not only because it gave her a chance to get everything off her chest that she'd been struggling with that week, but it provided accountability. The priest would give her "homework" to do as well, guiding her in guarding her thoughts, helping her to put what she was feeling in perspective, and moving her to regaining the spiritual life she'd neglected leading up to and during the affairs.

I offered her some direction as well. One of the key task I gave her early on was to memorize Psalm 51. This is the Psalm that King David wrote after having his own discovery day with the prophet Nathaniel. Not only had he taken another man's wife, but had her husband indirectly murdered by commanding he was put on the front lines in a battle to ensure his death. While he had to face the consequences of what he'd done, God forgave him. That psalm documents his repentance.

I knew in the coming months, if she progressed as she should, that she would face a lot of guilt. My hope was this Psalm, drilled into her head, would ensure that she didn't give into despair. Sure enough, at about four months from discovery day, she for the first time felt the responsibility of what she had done, and for the next nine months, she cried everyday over the guilt she felt. True repentance set in. Through her tears, God cleansed her soul over a period of months.

At first, it was hard for her to approach God again, after what she'd done. But I credit much of her progress with the rest of re-building to her spiritual work on herself, and God's grace working in what she offered. She faced her guilt head on. She acknowledged it. She repented of it. She didn't run from it.

She also started going with me to all extra services. She developed the ear to really listen to the words of the services, hear and think about what was said in all the hymns and readings. Like most of us, she'd allowed the words to flow in one ear and out the other way too easily. Many times the services spoke to her heart. Certain prayers would speak to what she dealt with. Especially those services involv-ing a saint who had committed adultery took on new meaning and support for her.

She began praying daily. Cleaning houses often meant having plenty of alone time. So aside from her rule of prayer, she would of-ten have expanded prayer times during the day as opportunity presented itself. Through this, she hashed out a lot of what she faced with God. One of the key disciplines God gave her was to focus on five main areas of spiritual healing: humility, repentance, thankful-ness, faithfulness, and service. By keeping these goals in sight, it guided her spiritual recovery.

If there was one activity that gave me the most hope that she wouldn't be as likely to return to her affair mindset, it was her invest-ment in rebuilding her spiritual life. As she found out during the affair, it is near impossible to be so focused on God and one's rela-tionship with Him, and allow such flagrant sin to dominate one's life at the same time. The more I knew her spiritual life was growing and thriving, the less of a threat I felt that she would return to the pig trough.

My Healing

Up to this point, I've mainly discussed Lenita's healing process. So I can hear you saying, "But what happened with your healing?" While my healing is in large part dependent upon her healing, there were things I needed to do as well if I were to heal. If I wanted to give Lenita every chance to save the marriage, then it would be counterproductive for her to do everything right, and I still not be able to heal and rebuild. It takes two to rebuild a marriage. If either spouse fails to participate, the end will be failure.

Unfortunately, a lot of hurt spouses fail to understand this. It is easy to see that the unfaithful spouse cheated, he did the damage, now it is his job to fix it. To a large extent, this is true. But if the hurt spouse doesn't put in the effort as well, then there is little the unfaithful spouse can do to repair the marriage and the hurt spouse. It is called a marriage because it means you are in this together, for better or for worse. This is part of the "worse." Though you didn't cause him to cheat, aren't to blame for his cheating, nor did you deserve the pain your spouse caused, you still have a necessary part to play in the rebuilding, if indeed rebuilding is your goal. If it isn't, then you might as well approach it that way up front rather than pretend to want it while sabotaging the unfaithful spouse's work.

Note, it may take three months or so once discovering the affair to get past the roller coaster of emotions enough to start working on yourself. No problem. One has to exit crisis mode, get out of intensive care before focusing on these things. How long that takes for any one individual will be different. Here are the areas I believed helped me to heal and rebuild with Lenita, keeping in mind that I healed faster than most do.

Attitude

Your outlook has a lot to do with how well you can rebuild as the hurt spouse. There were several attitudes that I think helped me heal as fast as I did.

Empathy. Did I experience hurt and loss? You bet. Nothing I'm saying here diminishes that reality. That said, I did, from the very beginning, have a sense of empathy for my wife. My first thoughts upon reading that log was realizing her soul was in danger of separation from God. For the first time in our married life, I feared that we would not spend eternity together. I realized if she was going to be restored, it would likely be through me. If I didn't cooperate, she could be spiritually lost. Yes, God could have accomplished her healing without me, but it would have been harder for Lenita to respond if she lost me and our marriage, and she would likely live in the pig pen for the rest of her life.

Love. Most people don't understand what love really is. They think it is a feeling, passion, friendship, or whatever. Those are all part of what real love is. But what many take as love is selfish in nature. "I like how he makes me feel!" "I've never felt so alive with anyone before!" This is the basis for most unfaithfulness. At the core of it all is someone strokes their ego, treats them like a king or queen, and they *feel* loved.

True love is not dependent upon feelings or what I can get out of the relationship, but is willing to sacrifice one's self for the other, is not dependent upon circumstances or even what the other person has done. This is why the Bible verse, "For God so loved the world..." is so powerful. God loved the world despite repeated rejection of Him. I felt my love for my wife would never change. No matter what she did. That's not to say her actions wouldn't have consequences, even as God lets us suffer the consequences of our own sins. If Lenita hadn't responded as she did, had fought the rebuilding, and we had ended up in divorce, I would have still love her even as I hated what she had done and the suffering I would have dealt with.

I'm not saying my love for her didn't have its selfish components, but because I had a love for her that didn't change based on how good she was, I wanted to give every chance to heal her and our relationship. It gave me the desire to see rebuilding happen and the empathy to help her find that healing. Because my love for her was unchanging, I was ready and willing to give 100% to rebuilding, and work to make sure I gave her every chance I could to find her own healing.

Commitment. I knew both from common sense and from articles I'd read that rebuilding wasn't an easy road. I knew it would take years, not weeks or months. I had no illusions that we'd be back to normal within the year, or even two. We would be making life-altering changes to our relationship. I knew from experience it would require a time of identity crisis that would feel "not normal" for at least a year, more likely two, assuming no falling off the wagon occurred. I knew for me, life was about to change big time. I had no idea if I'd be happy with the new life or not.

But I knew one thing. I loved her and had invested 29 years and three kids of my life into her. I wasn't about to let that go without a fight. My main goal was to say, if the marriage ultimately failed, that I had given it my all. I didn't want to think, "If only I had done" this or that, maybe the marriage could have been saved.

So I went into rebuilding focused on doing all that I could to, 1) make sure I didn't stall out in my own healing process, 2) not get in the way of her healing process, and 3) be willing to make the changes I needed to make for the healing of the marriage.

Without developing these attitudes, rebuilding will be hampered. There is a rule when talking about computer speed: your computer will only go as fast as its slowest component. You can have a blazing fast processor and gigs of memory, but if your hard drive is slow or your internet connection is slow, it drags the whole system down. Same with rebuilding. If either spouse fails to work at rebuilding, then it doesn't happen.

Triggers

One of the issues many hurt spouses have are triggers: events, people, or objects that trigger memories of the affair and its accompanying pain. A hurt spouse doesn't realize how many triggers lie in wait for him. The car used in the affair can be a trigger. Often that car needs to be sold, but even then, every car with the same make, model, and color on the road can be a trigger. If discovery day or any affair event happened around a holiday, that becomes a trigger. Sex often becomes a trigger as well for many.

How did I deal with these? I think it was in part my personality, but also several mental outlooks I had which minimized the effect of triggers during rebuilding. Don't get me wrong, I had some, but not as much as many hurt spouses tend to report. I don't think you can ever totally get away from it. For me, since discovery day happened four days before our anniversary, memories of the affair will always be linked to that celebration. Here are steps I took to minimize the effect of triggers.

Reclaim. Early on, I began reclaiming what was mine, like my wife, but also reclaiming the activities that her and the affair partner participated in.

A key example is the gym where Lenita met Bubba and their relationship grew. That first week as we sorted through the issues, I had two options about her and the gym. I could demand that she end her membership there and no longer go to the gym, or I could start going with her. I knew if I told her to end her membership, she'd do it, but it would be a loss for her. There were enough losses for her to deal with in all this, I didn't need to add more unnecessarily.

But two things sold me on going to the gym with her instead. 1) Going with her provided a great activity to spend more time together. 2) She had developed memories with Bubba there. That was their place. I wanted to overwrite those memories with new one's, with me. What I didn't take into account is how this effectively erased the gym as a trigger. If I'd not done that, every time I drove by the gym it would have reminded me of the affairs. Now, it reminds me of the fun Lenita and I have enjoyed together.

Yes, I know what you're thinking. 3) I needed the exercise. More than I realized at the time.

I will admit that the first time or two there, I felt very uncomfortable. Every action she did I could see in my mind's eye that she did it with Bubba. But in facing it down and reclaiming it, within a couple of weeks, it had become our place, not theirs, and I erased a possible trigger.

Guarding my thoughts. Another aspect is what you focus on. There is a good story floating around in our support group of late. An old man told a young boy that within each person there are two wolves fighting to gain control over us. A good wolf and a bad wolf. The boy asked, "Which one wins?" The old man said, "The wolf you feed."

It would have been easy to let myself get wrapped up in the pain every time a trigger ran across my path. Sometimes I did. But in part because of my personality and/or making an effort to not focus on them, most of the time when a trigger registered in my thoughts, I noticed it, then moved onto other thoughts. I didn't stop what I was doing and spend the next few minutes brooding over it. I didn't feed it.

Early after discovery day, this will be harder to do. All you can do is thinking about the affair nonstop, 24/7. But once the roller coaster winds down to a manageable level, learning to let the trigger pass you by without meditating on it is key to not letting those triggers control your life.

A good example in my situation was our sex life. One time thoughts of the affair partner being with my wife caused excitement to die off and prematurely end our connect time. But most of the time, my thoughts stayed on what was happening at the moment, not wandering around in imaginations of what might have happened. Simply put, don't feed that wolf. Starve him and eventually he'll go away.

Find positive meaning. This is especially important for holidays or events that are linked to the affair, as mine is with our anniversary. There's no getting around it, our anniversary is always going to remind me of the affairs. There are two routes I can take. I can let those painful memories define the celebration and destroy it, or I can invest new meaning into that celebration that defines discovery day.

I chose the later. As our one-year anniversary of discovery day approached, along with our 30th wedding anniversary, I decided that I would take the approach to celebrate the fact that we'd made it to our 30th. On our 29th anniversary, I had no idea if we'd still be married by our 30th. Or if we were, if we would be happy or not. The fact that we were not only still married, but doing well rebuilding and loved each other more than ever was reason to celebrate making it to our one-year discovery day celebration.

Because of how the days fell, our anniversary was in the middle of the week, while our discovery day anniversary was on Friday. So we made the choice to celebrate our thirtieth anniversary on our discovery day anniversary instead of pushing to the next weekend as a way to take the bite out of that day.

I commemorated the day by deleting emails I'd kept of her and Bubba's conversations. She thought she'd deleted them, but she had only moved them to the trash folder and never emptied it. So I copied their emails to a separate folder before deleting her trash bin. I'd only looked through them two or three times during that year. Doing so was painful as there were at least two or three where they discuss their love and lovemaking.

I'm not sure why I kept them. Divorce never became a real issue.

Texas has no-fault divorces, but also adultery can be used to divorce with fault too. I'd never thought seriously about divorce, though I knew it was a possibility if things headed south. But the emails would have been some proof that it had happened, if I needed it. So the act of deleting them was a step of faith on my part, and a message to her that she'd done a lot to rebuild my trust in the past year and that she was going to continue down that path.

From here on out, yes, I will remember the affair on our wedding anniversary, but I'll also be thankful for the love we have and how far we've come from those days of marital crisis. By investing it with new meaning, we've minimized that trigger's negative effect on me.

Initially, triggers are like a wild horse. It may take some doing, but they can be tamed. What you want to do is define them, rather than them defining you and enslaving you in their grip.

Depression

Depression is one of the five stages of grief, right before acceptance. So while depression is. . . depressing, it also means the beginning of the end is in sight.

In the early days after discovery day, I wasn't depressed, rather I was first in shock, then fearful, then finding it hard to believe I was experiencing this, reeling from the loss of our relationship, and so many other emotions, often within the span of a few minutes. There was a sense of depression mixed in with it all, but the other emotions didn't allow it to gain a big foothold, so I didn't notice it as much.

Also, once we got past the crisis of the first four weeks and it appeared she was headed in the right directions, and I began to see progress, I became more and more thankful. My worst fears of her leaving me faded into the depths of possibilities with each passing day.

Once the crisis was over, we experienced what many couples in this situation do: hysterical bonding. Each spouse, fearful of losing the other one, focuses their full attention to making the other person happy. In effect, your dating days come alive again. For most couples, this last around two to three months. Others may go longer. But eventually you come down off that infatuation-like passion and the negative emotions of the affair returns to haunt you.

If we hysterical bonded, and I think we did, it was hard to tell.

One characteristic of hysterical bonding is wanting lots of sex. But we'd already been in that mode since her affairs started, and even to date it has slowed down a bit, but not by much. So we never had a clear picture of when it began and ended based on that metric. That may have something to do with our work on the marriage. But during this time, depression is distant. The relationship is exciting again. Both of you are totally focused on each other, just like when you dated.

I know pretty much when my depression hit me. About nine months after discovery day, I began lamenting what I'd lost. The purity of our relationship, the trust I'd had in her before the affairs, the never-settled question of "how could she do this to me?" During that period, I read her and Bubba's emails to each other. I allowed myself to brood over what had happened, and feared the coming discovery day anniversary. I had read so many couples that did fine until that time, and then it all fell apart. Would something blindside me around that time and derail all we'd worked for?

Ironically, what I was experiencing is what happens to many couples in approaching their one-year mark. Often either or both spouses expect to be over the affairs by the one year mark. When they are not, it may seem it will never happen. Many get stuck in depression, and it drags down the hurt spouse, and makes healing difficult. They lose hope in rebuilding, and decide to cut their losses. Or they consign themselves to a "loveless marriage" because the hurt spouse doesn't feel they have other options, so they stay depressed for months or years.

Selfishly, I also lamented what I had lost with my old life. In my pre-affair days, I rarely ever did the dishes. I had all my free time to devote to my writing. I didn't have to go to the grocery store, the gym, to watch fireworks if I didn't want to on the fourth, and I was free to buy what I wanted without needing to pass it through her. I had my own private life. But no more. That was all gone. Now a lot of the time I would have spent writing and critiquing other writers and marketing, I spent with Lenita.

It sounds bad on this side of the fence, and it was. It had been bad for years. I was selfish. I'd lived in my own world with Lenita's paralleling mine for so long, it was comfortable. It was familiar. What I was doing at that point still felt "not me." Instead, it felt like a pair of jeans I had tried on and grew tired of, wanting my old comfortable jeans with the hole in the knee back. But it was gone, and I couldn't get it back.

One point during that time, I expressed my desires to Lenita. Not so much to make her feel I didn't want her, but because she should know what I was going through. She asked me if I'd rather have that life back. I shook my head. "No, that was my selfish life that needs to die, no matter how much I liked it." I knew after some time had passed, my desire for the old life would pass too. I recognized it was part of the process of reforming my identity to incorporate the new life into my "normal." But it did contribute to my depression.

After about a month to two months of growing depression, one day I said to myself, "It's gone, it's over. There's no point in focusing on what you've lost. It's in the past. All you have is the future. That won't be better if you sit around feeling sorry for yourself for the rest of your life." I realized at that point I was feeding the wrong wolf. That is when my depression started to end and acceptance of what happened solidified into reality. That is when I could move on.

Writing

I'm a published science fiction/fantasy writer under the pen name of R. L. Copple (http://www.rlcopple.com). When discovery day hit, I'd been working on the serialization of a novel. I had published the individual stories to that point, with the intent to compile them into a full novel once done. But when the discovery of Lenita's affairs hit me, my writing life ground to a halt. For three months, the only writing I did was for a monthly column I had pledged to write. I didn't touch anything during that period. My whole focus was on dealing with the fallout from the affairs.

Then in July of 2011, a little over two months after discovery day, I was released from my job. Not only did I have the recovery from the affair on my mind, now I worried about our future finances.

Toward the end of August, 2011, I finally pulled myself up enough to finish editing a book I'd written some years ago, and had been editing forever. I did the work to get cover art, and published it myself.

In September, I had an idea for a non-fiction book. As a pastor, I'd written plenty of non-fiction type work, but never published any of it. Now I wanted to gather the experience I'd gained in creating ebooks and put that into a book others could buy. So I put my efforts into writing, editing, and publishing that for the next three months. By the end of November, I had an ebook titled: *How to Make an Ebook: Using Free Software.* To date, it has been my best seller.

Still, despite the activity, I couldn't bring myself to sit down and write any creative fiction. I wrote blog post, non-fiction titles, edited and published books, but no new fiction stories. I began to worry that my fiction writing career would grind to a halt once I edited and published the last title I had in the queue unless I got over this hesitancy to write fiction.

But I'd done plenty of writing about affairs. On the support group I'm on, they had a journal function. Writing helps me to sort out my thinking. I'm a big picture guy. If I can see the whole, then I can understand the meaning and function of the parts. My mind has always thought that way. So journaling about what had happened, telling my story, became its own therapy, along with getting input from other people.

Additionally, on the forums, I dug into helping people through their affairs. I'm a quick learner, and once I see the bigger picture, it is easy for me to see where someone's individual situation fits, and how to help them. Additionally, it was therapeutic for my own journey because it added meaning to what I was going through. It meant I had a hand in helping other people get through this ordeal and even save marriages.

I jumped into that role so early in the process, as I tend to do on any forum I'm on, some I think began questioning whether my wife really had an affair and whether I was there to get ego strokes. I'm sure at times I came across as a Mr. Know-it-all. But that only flared up one time, and my assurances that I've been in pain and have gone through my wife's affair was not some made up story to become one of the gang for some nefarious purpose. Rather, it helped me to heal, to help others through what I'd gone through.

For me, learning how to deal with something, whether it is creating an ebook or rebuilding a marriage, is knowledge to be shared so that I can help others. Otherwise, I'm being selfish. Especially when it comes to something like infidelity. Most people don't want to tell the whole world about it like I'm doing with this book.

So I wrote plenty of non-fiction posts, blog posts, journals, but no creative fiction. Not one story.

That changed in December of 2011. I like to give my blog readers the Christmas present of a short story on my blog each year. So I pulled myself together long enough to write the first piece of fiction in eight months. A short story based upon my *Virtual Chronicles* world.

I thought, "Good, I've finally written something. Maybe now it will start flowing again." But it didn't. For most of 2012, I still didn't write any fiction. When my one-year discovery day anniversary passed, and I'd gone for over a year with that one, lone flash fiction to show for my fiction writing, I really began to get worried. I thought for sure I would have been over it enough to get back to writing again. I still edited and published work, but to paraphrase Elron from *Lord of the Rings*, my list of books grew thin. I only had two left and one of them needed some major editing.

I tried to evaluate why I was having trouble getting back to writing. I had some theories but no solid, "Ah, yes, that's it." The most likely theory involved an internal fear of losing myself into my own writing world. Since I started writing fiction at the end of 2005, I invested every moment I could in learning writing, editing, and collaborating with other writers. It was my world, and Lenita wasn't part of it.

When Lenita started her affair, I was deep into writing two new books. Aside from my utter disbelief that she'd ever be unfaithful to me, the warning signs I did get I quickly dismissed. I was so focused on my writing, I ignored flares that if I'd been more attentive, I might have paid more attention to. So I think one reason is the fear if I got sucked back into my writing world, I'd return to that mode of thinking, she'd fall off the wagon, and I wouldn't notice it for a few months, again.

But I also think I partially blamed my writing career on what happened. I blamed spending every spare minute on writing, ignoring her desire for me to go with her to the grocery store, not going to the gym with her because I didn't want to "waste" time I could be writing. I had ignored her, and to some extent, God as well. I feared if I started writing again, I would find myself ignoring what was really important. Because when I do something, I get really focused on it to the point of exclusion of everything else.

The reality is, however, that I needed to find balance. Which involves making sure what is important is established first. With the passing of months, it is ironic that on the two year mark of when Lenita began her affair with Clyde in October 2010, in October of 2012 I wrote my second short story for a Halloween gift and put it on my blog.

Immediately after that, in November, I participated in "National Novel Writing Month" as I had done every year since 2006. I'd written most of my novels that way. The only year I didn't participate much was in 2011. I did do less than a week on a new book, but quit to focus on the how to make an ebook, book. It was the first year since I'd participated that I didn't write more than 50,000 words on a novel.

But in 2012, for the first time in two years, I wrote a full novel, the third in the *Virtual Chronicles* series. I'm writing this section of this book less than a month from finishing that book. Lenita reports not feeling neglected during that time, and I do feel a release from the block I had. I'm expecting I'll be able to write more in 2013 now that balance has been achieved. The fear that I'll end up in the same spot again if I write is subsiding.

If anything I've learned through this process, it is to prioritize your time. I had gone almost six years ignoring my wife's needs because I wanted to make it in writing. But what joy is there in becoming a best selling author if your marriage and family have fallen apart in the meantime? Meaningless. With a more balanced life, I may not be able to move as fast as I want with my writing, but I will move forward. And I'll still have a loving wife and exciting marriage when I get there.

Healing the Marriage

Infidelity does one of two things to a marriage. It either destroys it or makes it stronger. Note, I didn't say it would be either divorce or rebuild. Going through a divorce can make a person stronger. Couples can rebuild but find their marriage is never as vibrant as it once was. Annoyances you used to put up with now seem unbearable.

Whether one goes through separation or divorce, the real question is whether the relationship does more than survive, but thrives. The problem in many cases is that the unfaithful spouse thinks once it blows over, things will eventually get back to "normal" and over time, the marriage will be as good as it ever was. Meanwhile, the hurt spouse tends to not even want to think about working on his part of the marriage, not until he is over the affair. In both cases, the marriage is left to flounder because neither couple is working on it.

For sure, in the early weeks after discovery day, the hurt spouse will generally not be able to focus on fixing the part he played in any marital problems. As mentioned before, first the hurt spouse needs to be released from intensive care. However, no hurt spouse can wait for two or more years to address these problems if rebuilding is expected to succeed either.

For that same reason, the unfaithful spouse cannot expect the hurt spouse to get out of intensive care if he doesn't allow them to heal by failing to be transparent, honest, humble, totally committed to rebuilding, and all we've discussed. If it takes the unfaithful spouse two years to start freely discussing the affairs with their spouse, facing the guilt and dealing with it, then that is when the hurt spouse can finally get out of intensive care and focus on the marriage. But by then, it could be too little, too late.

Why? For one simple reason. If the marriage is not better than it was before the affair, the resulting "new normal" will feel inadequate. If the couple ends up with the same problems continuing after the affair as before, they'll ask themselves, "For what am I going through the pain of rebuilding if the marriage isn't going to get better?" How happy a couple are after going through rebuilding will in large part depend on whether marital problems were addressed and solved during the period of rebuilding.

We'll discuss this more in the 4th part of this book, but among other things, one of the main reasons I think our rebuilding went so smoothly as it did and was so successful is because we not only worked on repairing the effects of the affairs, but repairing our marital relationship. Through the process, we felt more in love with one another, and that love gave us the emotional motivation to struggle through the pain of rebuilding. What we've built in response to the affairs is in many ways a stronger marriage than we had before the affairs.

We started working on our marriage early in the process. I went to our counseling session for the first time, two weeks after returning from our 29th wedding anniversary. Lenita had gone by herself the first week. After I got my story off my chest, my wife asked about the sex addict issue. The counselor determined that Lenita's situation wasn't a sex addiction problem, but a marital problem.

To some extent, in retrospect, it was more than that. The counselor never delved into Lenita's need for attention and affirmation that she'd had all her life. The attention the affair partners had given her was in large part what had fueled her addictive reaction to their advances. That said, a lot of what she said was still true, because one of the reasons their attention was so exciting was because I wasn't giving her much on a regular basis. The reason I wasn't giving her much attention went back to some of the issues I discussed at the beginning of this book.

At first, I worried that focusing on the marital issues would be, in effect, placing blame for her affairs on me as much as her. But the counselor never went there, and early on I gained some insight that I've discussed before. That my blame for the marital problems contributed to the temptation for her to cheat, but the responsibility for going outside the marriage to address those problems was entirely hers. It was an improper and destructive response to marital problems. It is, in effect, seeing there is a fire, and deciding to throw gasoline on it instead of water.

So our counselor wanted us to stop reading the book on sexual addiction that we'd been reading, and get *His Needs, Her Needs: How to Affair Proof Your Marriage* by Willard F. Jr. Harley. We did and began reading. One of his opening points is that when couples experiencing infidelity came to him for help, and he began focusing on these romantic needs to fill what he calls the love bank, which in turn gives each spouse a feeling of being in love, his success rate in helping couples to rebuild went from around 40% into the 60% range.

The reason for this is very obvious. When you both feel in love with each other, it makes it a whole ton easier to rebuild and helps rebuild the trust faster. It gives the unfaithful spouse the motivation to cut off ties with the affair partner(s) and the hurt spouse the power to work through the pain and get a foothold in the relationship. It is in effect not saying the marital problems were the cause of the affair, but that they are part of the healing from the affair.

To put it bluntly, the book drastically changed our relationship. She learned what she'd been doing all of our marriage that said to me, "I don't love you," and likewise I learned what I had failed to do to show her I loved her. We hadn't been making the other person feel important to the other. So while we always thought we had a great marriage, in reality it was weak. We loved each other, but were not showing that love to each other effectively.

As a result, we instituted some major changes. We started doing more together. I went with her to the grocery store. I went to the gym with her and we swam together three to five nights a week. She started going with me to the Vespers church service, both because she had to go to confession and it gave us more time to read the books together. Even though she doesn't need to go to confession weekly any longer, she still comes and she still reads a book in the car there and back. She made a commitment to continue having regular sex with me and treating me as important, with respect. Once unemployed, I helped her with her jobs on occasion. I made a big deal of Valentine's Day, and participated in the Fourth of July and Halloween activities I'd always avoided.

As mentioned before, we went from spending around one or two hours a week together to well over twenty hours a week. We both realigned our priorities to what was really important in maintaining a vibrant love in our marriage. Not only a commitment to love, but making each other feel loved through actions.

At first, it felt like I was giving up my comfort zone for a life of sacrifice. I could no longer selfishly hunker down in my room and do what I wanted. But I knew if we were to be married, then we had to really be married. That is, united not just in an abstract love, but a concrete love that says, "You're the most important person in my life." That required letting her into my life, and her to let me into hers. We could no longer be satisfied living parallel marital lives. We had to be united fully into one in all ways.

Now I wouldn't trade these changes for anything. I treasure the time I spend with my wife. While I'm not able to get as much done as I used to, what is more important? Making sure Lenita knows I love her and keeping the love-fires burning, or getting that next book written one or two months sooner? Obviously the former.

Currently, I don't think I've sacrificed much in giving up my private life, not nearly as much as I've gained. At first, I felt it was. I had no idea if I'd always be looking back and longing for the way it was before the affairs. But I don't. Not that I am glad the affair happened, mind you, but I'm glad that with God's help, we made something good out of the mess we were in. We used the infidelity to build a stronger marriage instead of settling for the same old way it was or ending in divorce.

A lot of the reason that happened is because we didn't hesitate to work on the marriage even during some of my most painful weeks, and continued to do so. Both couples have to be committed for rebuilding to work. If one or the other doesn't do their part, the chances of successful rebuilding go way down.

The Future

The above is the story of how Lenita allowed temptation to gain a foothold in her life and cause great harm to our marriage, myself, and our children. But it is also a story of her repentance, and how she healed and continues to heal not only herself, but me, the marriage, and our family, exhibiting a great love in the process through the grace of God. A person doesn't go through the pain and suffering she has in healing without a great love to make the sacrifice.

As I write this, we are over 20 months from discovery day. Not quite two years. While I feel secure that Lenita won't stray on me again, I still have moments of fear. Triggers pop up occasionally and I fear the worst, even if I have no evidence. However, those have become less and less frequent as I've gone down this road.

While I have that confidence, I'm also aware that the possibility looms on the horizon that she might be tempted and fall again. I'm even aware if I'm not careful, if I allow myself to cross boundaries because I think, "I'll never cheat on Lenita," I could find myself in the same boat as her.

She says herself that I'm not the only one whose trust has been damaged from the affair, but her ability to trust herself. In truth, this is a healthy mistrust. It keeps us from seeing how close to the edge of the cliff we can get without falling off. Because once you've fallen, it's too late. Not having blind trust in each other or ourselves will be what prevents the next occurrence.

Several items give me hope for the future. Lenita has returned to herself. I could see her moving out of the fog as time progressed and she worked on herself. She no longer can stay awake for long past midnight like she did in the midst of the affair. While she is not the same person as before the affair, thankfully, she is more like the woman I knew.

Also, Lenita—and I by extension—have learned our lesson concerning our marriage. We've learned to treat each other as the most important person in our lives. Our relationship is more vibrant and alive than it was in the first year of our marriage. Even better in some regards. We know what to avoid, and neither her nor I will be taking each other for granted or treat boundaries as an inconvenience.

We both look forward to growing old together. Yet this must be said. Should it come to it, and two, three, five, ten or more years later, she or I have an affair after this book has been published, it won't be because what we've stated here is wrong, doesn't work, or flawed. It will be because somewhere down the line, we failed to continue doing what we've stated here, and allowed temptation to gain a foothold in our lives. So even though at this moment, I don't see either of us having an affair again into the future, if it does happen, it doesn't invalidate what we are sharing with you.

To that end, now that you have our story, we want to share with you what we've learned from our time going through these events and from others in a more organized manner. The following parts of this book contain articles I wrote that deal with healing from the affairs. It distills what we've learned in digestible chunks. Lenita had more of a hand in the writing of the "Healing Steps for the Unfaithful Spouse." It is our hope that others can learn from our mistakes and successes through our rebuilding from the devastation of infidelity.

Part 2 – For the Unfaithful Spouse

Healing Steps for the Unfaithful Spouse

This chapter is for those unfaithful spouses who wish to rebuild their marriages after having committed an act of infidelity. Many unfaithful spouses who have ended an affair and want to save their marriage don't always know what they need to do, what approach they should have, or understand fully the damage to the hurt spouse. Usually, the "natural" reaction is the wrong one to successfully rebuild. My wife, Lenita, who is an unfaithful spouse and has successfully rebuilt our marriage, wrote an article on what the unfaithful spouse needs to do to help the hurt spouse heal. I'm taking the core outline from that article to write this chapter.

This chapter assumes that you have told your hurt spouse about the affair and that he knows the general details of the affair. If he doesn't know about your affair, be sure to read the next chapter, "Should I Tell?" Because, until you do and reveal all relevant details, no matter how hurtful to him, healing the marriage will not happen. The next chapter will focus on why, when, and how to tell.

But assuming you have told the hurt spouse about all needed details of the affair, what are the ways in which you can best help you and your hurt spouse heal and save the marriage, if indeed that is your goal? Here are the main areas that need your attention.

1) Be prepared to invest yourself 100% and more into the rebuilding of the marriage. That means two major points. One, rebuilding will not be easy, especially for the unfaithful spouse. To help your spouse heal means facing the pain of what you've done, examining it, and dealing with it until the wound has healed. These are hard things for anyone to do. Unless you are totally committed to doing whatever it takes, you will tend to falter when, for instance, you debate whether to tell your spouse about that chance encounter with the affair partner or not.

Two, realize this will take years, not weeks. Too often the unfaithful spouse wants to put it all behind them. He doesn't want it thrown into his face regularly. That is understandable. But keep in mind that while you have known this secret for weeks, months, or even years, for the spouse it is fresh and new information that has to be processed, the loss grieved over, and the trust that has been violated to be rebuilt over several months. To do that, he needs to talk about it, deal with it, and process it to the point of satisfaction that he can move past it. That will not happen quickly. Doing the following will help it to happen as quickly as possible, but even in the best of circumstances, don't expect everything to be "back to normal" until a minimum of two years. In some cases it may take even longer. No two individuals are the same. But unless you realize you are in it for the long haul, it will be easy to get discouraged when after three or four months, he is still bringing up issues about the affair. He has to deal with the affair, and if he isn't allowed to, then he is prevented from healing.

2) Develop an attitude of healing. Lenita listed several examples of what that attitude needed to be:

I will own up to what I have done and place none of the blame on anyone else.

I will never try to 'gag' you but will listen bravely without flinching away and answer/discuss anything you need to, anytime you need to.

I will be humble.

I will show you my heart.

I will understand that I must be responsible for helping you heal and that I must work diligently to heal myself.

I will not be defensive concerning the affair or the affair partner.

Without these attitudes, the chances of rebuilding are slim. This is because for healing the marriage to take place, the bulk of the work will be with the unfaithful spouse. The bottom line is you have hurt your spouse, and now it is your job to heal that hurt. You are the only one who can heal your spouse, because only you can rebuild the trust that has been stolen from them. To not do the above is the equivalent of shutting the door on the marriage. If you said to point #1, "Yes, I am committed," then this needs to be the first place you take a stand. Because if you approach it with any other attitude, the following steps will not only be harder, but you'll not implement them as fully as you should to really heal your spouse.

3) Break all contact with the affair partner. Until the hurt spouse feels secure that there is no more contact of any kind going on between you and your affair partner, for him, the affair isn't over. As long as that door is still open, however slightly, the hurt spouse will live in fear that if the affair hasn't restarted, it is only a matter of time until it does. Contact means the emotional bonds are still alive. Only complete and utter no contact will allow the hurt spouse the ability to start healing. To not do so magnifies the odds against any rebuilding efforts being permanent.

Unfortunately, this is one step many unfaithful spouses find hard to follow through on. Especially if they were caught while the affair was ongoing. It usually means a sudden end to a relationship that at that moment, neither of you were ready to end. Maybe one goodby phone call and then to never speak or see them again sounds harsh and drastic. When someone has fallen in love with another person, even if inappropriately, to stop all contact is the equivalent to saying to the affair partner, "I don't love you, leave me alone and never talk to me again," when that is the exact opposite of how you feel. Yet if you want the affair to be over for your spouse so that healing of the marriage can begin, this is a necessity.

Remind yourself that if you are experiencing the sudden loss of a relationship with someone you were with for a few days, weeks, or months, how much more is your spouse going through when they are feeling the loss of a relationship they've had for years with you? At this point, you have to chose and invest yourself in whichever path you wish to go. In either case, that means cutting off all contact with the other you are leaving. No matter how much you love him. Bottom line: this is one of the hard consequences of allowing yourself to have an affair.

"But I work with the affair partner. How do I deal with that?" You may find your spouse is one of the rare ones who can deal with that situation, but with 99% of the hurt spouses, even if they acknowledge the financial stress of losing a job you've held for years, maybe nearing retirement, and the unpredictability of finding new work, the chances of successfully rebuilding the marriage goes down drastically if continued contact of any kind is retained.

Until contact is cut off, the affair is still going for the hurt spouse, even if in truth it isn't. The hurt spouse has no means to know you are being faithful even while making frequent contact at work. He has no way to know you aren't meeting in a closet or room or car. He has no assurance that you aren't sharing lunches together and discussing personal issues. Rebuilding trust in a situation like that is next to impossible. It's like telling someone to put out the fire with water while you continue to blast it with a flame thrower.

As Lenita often told me when she faced something painful, "I asked for this, you didn't." When you allowed an affair to happen, you put at risk everything. Your marriage, your children, your job, your stability. There may come a point that you have to sacrifice your job security for marital security. That can be one of the costs of having and affair. Which will you chose?

There may be solutions. You can ask for a transfer from your department if the company is large enough. Preferably to another building. Your spouse would even by happy in most cases to hear the transfer meant a move to another town. But if that doesn't work out, and there is no choice but to either quit or stay in contact with the person, it may mean making that hard choice to find another job. We again go back to points #1 and #2. It may mean less money, or financial hardships. That's when you have to ask what is more important to you? Your marriage or your job? If it comes down to a decision between the two, and no compromise can be worked out, it may mean making a decision of which one to sacrifice. No contact is that important.

No contact also extends to mementos you have from your affair partner. Pictures, written letters, emails, or other items bought for you all constitute links to the affair partner. These should be deleted or thrown away to complete non-contact. Both because they can be triggers to the hurt spouse, but also triggers for you, causing you to recall him or her and the "good" times. The goal of no contact is to let the affair partner fade into the past, so you can focus on your spouse, your marriage, and your family.

4) Become totally transparent. What is meant by this is to open yourself up in all ways that relate to rebuilding trust in the aftermath of the affair, so that your spouse can see everything he needs to see to feel secure that contact is not still ongoing, and that you are being truthful.

Think of it like this. The hurt spouse just discovered that you've broken your wedding vows to him, and in most cases lied about it, hid it from him. You've stolen something precious to him: his trust in you and his security in your love for him. Any "secret," any request for "privacy" to him is translated that you have something more to hide about the affair. He has no reason to trust you at this point.

It will take months of constantly discovering that you are telling the truth to begin to trust that you are actually doing that. The only way he can see you telling the truth is by being transparent.

There is a saying, that trust takes a lifetime to build, but seconds to destroy. Trust is the glue that holds a marriage together. By opening yourselves to each other in the most intimate of ways, you have made yourself vulnerable to being hurt. Trust means "I trust you enough not to hurt me. So I open my soul to you." The moment that perceived truth is broken by being hurt, the natural reaction is to pull back and not trust. After many positive examples of truth-telling, gradually he will start to trust again. Even then, it will never be the same innocent trust he had prior to the affair. Like an accident victim, he will tend to flinch inwardly when anything that even looks like the same threat darkens his path. That will be with him to some degree for the rest of his life. The only way to rebuild that trust is to no longer hide anything from your spouse that would be of concern to him or her.

What does "no longer hide anything" mean? We're not talking telling him what you ate for lunch, or all the thoughts that go through your mind everyday. Rather, there are two questions you can ask yourself that will determine if it is something you should tell him: "If I were him, would I want to know this?" and "Is this something I don't want him to know?" If you answer "yes" to either of those questions, then to be transparent, you should tell him.

On the practical side, transparency translates into actions like giving your spouse the user names and passwords to all social media accounts you have. All email accounts. All cell phone's and their bills. When your spouse asks to look at them, you readily give them over without the need to "erase" anything. Likewise, one of the best trust rebuilding activities you can do is to tell him things he could have never discovered himself. For instance, my wife told me about any and all encounters with her affair partner, who for some months kept attempting to contact her. Most of those I would have never known about if she hadn't told me. But she wanted to be totally transparent with me. Having her tell me that aided in my rebuilding of trust in her.

Some spouses expect a level of privacy and are unwilling to give this up. However, this is unhealthy, even for a marriage that has not gone through an affair. Even more so once one spouse has hurt the other by having an affair. Some secrets a spouse has are harmless. Maybe you were called a nickname by family or friends when little, and you've never told your spouse out of embarrassment. Understandable. However, once a couple is married, the old saying, "No man is an island" takes on an increased meaning. Any activity you do can affect the marriage and relationship, and each spouse has the right to know about it. That right supersedes any rights to privacy a spouse may think they have. Bottom line, if you have information you don't want your spouse to know that affects the marriage in any way, financially, socially, emotionally, sexually, or spiritually, you don't have the right to keep that from him, and he has every right to find out, even spying, if he has probable cause.

Without consistent transparency, you severally limit the ability of the hurt spouse to rebuild trust in you and the marriage, and drastically lower the chance of success in rebuilding.

5) Avoid "rug sweeping" at all costs. There are two ways and motivations for wanting to take the issues generated by the affair and sweep them under the proverbial rug so you don't have to look at them or deal with them.

One, what you did is painful to face. It is easier to say, "Okay, that's in the past now. It's over. Time to move on," and clam up about the affair, expecting him to do the same. We've already discussed in the previous steps why this is dangerous. It prevents the hurt spouse from dealing with and healing from what has been done to him. He is not able to find closure. It also causes him to sense that you are continuing to hide something from him. Making it near impossible to rebuild trust again. Doing this will ensure the marriage will fail at some point because the hurt spouse will not heal.

Two, it also ensures that you, the unfaithful spouse, will not heal. You will help your hurt spouse heal in large part by healing yourself. He needs to know that you are working to not only discover what character issues as a person allowed you to treat any problems and fulfill any unmet needs in the marriage in such a destructive way, but that you are also working to fix those issues, to make the changes in yourself to prevent another occurrence from happening again.

If you refuse to face your issues and instead keep them out of sight, you will not heal. Indeed, by ignoring the need to face these issues and do the hard work to emotionally and spiritually heal yourself from this destructive event, the likelihood of it happening again is substantially higher. Your spouse knows this instinctively. If you are hiding from the issues, the fear that it will happen again is much greater than if he sees you wrestling with what you've done to him and yourself, and working to fix it.

6) Take advantage of counseling. Being willing to not only go to individual counseling to help you sort through your issues related to the affair, but also marital counseling, is a key component of healing for both of you. Especially important if your skills at communication are less than ideal. A counselor can help to facilitate constructive communication and conflict resolution. But even if you have good communication and you felt your marriage before the affair was good, this is still important.

For us, our marriage counselor helped point us in the right directions. Our first thought was my wife was dealing with a sexual addiction. But we didn't understand that term in its full clinical sense. Our counselor pointed us to where we needed to work on our marriage. I realized after the fact that claiming Lenita had a sexual addition was more a way to blame it on something rather than her bad choices. Self-diagnosis isn't a good idea. An objective, informed guide is much better for seeing where you are at and helping you through the maze of feelings and options you'll encounter.

That said, not all counselors are created equal. Many are not that experienced in dealing with infidelity. I've heard more than my share of stories where a counselor gave out bad advice. Sometimes enabling the unfaithful partner to violate many of the needed tasks listed above. If you have a counselor who does that, feel free to change. Not merely because they ask you to do hard things, but because they aren't helping one or both of you to heal. Get a second opinion. Find out if they have experience counseling couples involved in affairs. There is too much on the line to stick with someone out of some sense of loyalty to them if they are not helping either of you to heal.

7) Read books on dealing with the aftermath of affairs and marriage. For the unfaithful spouse, the following is required reading. Get a copy of *How To Help Your Spouse Heal From Your Affair: A Compact Manual For The Unfaithful* by Linda MacDonald. Read it, follow it. It is not a big book, but goes into much more detail than we can in this article. It is very practical, blunt, and tells you exactly what you as an unfaithful spouse needs to do to help you and your spouse heal. You don't need to have the hurt spouse read this book, though he certainly can if he wants. This book is for the unfaithful spouse, and is spot on in guiding you to what is needed if you wish to save the marriage.

After that book, I have three more highly recommended books for both of you to read. The first is *Getting Past the Affair: A Program to Help You Cope, Heal, and Move On -- Together or Apart* by Douglas K. Snyder. This book will take both of you through a process of healing, step by step. Very practical on issues like communication, and based on sound principles.

The second is *Not "Just Friends"* by Shirley Glass. This is the best book for gaining insight both into what happened in the affair for both parties, and the steps each needs to take to help heal from it. It is down to earth, easy to read, and very practical. The author has years of work in the field, and her understanding of the reasons why this happens and what needs to be done to change it are on target. Both spouses will greatly benefit reading this book.

The other is *His Needs, Her Needs: Building an Affair-Proof Marriage* by Willard F. Harley. This book attacks another issue that commonly plagues marriages that have gone through affairs: the need to show each other love in a way they understand it. Some people might balk at the idea of working on the marriage until the affair issues have been dealt with. But what Mr. Harley found out in his own counseling practice, is that the success of rebuilding was greatly increased when both spouses were able to effectively communicate the feeling of love to the other person.

If you think about it, it makes sense. The more in love you feel with your spouse, the more motivation you'll have to face all the hard tasks of rebuilding. Likewise, the more your spouse feels you love them, the more likely he'll be able to not only get past the damage of the affair easier, but also motivated to have empathy and forgiveness for what you did. Honest feelings of love become the oil in a marriage racked by an affair that speeds healing and makes all the efforts you do to rebuild that much more effective.

These last three books we suggest you read as a couple. Preferably reading to one another. This not only provides opportunity to bond and participate in an activity together, but provides many chances to explore the events of the affair in a non-threatening manner, and see them through the light of another person. You'll find out your "unique" experience isn't all that unique.

Once done with these, seek out other books. Not just about affairs, but marriage enrichment in general as well. It will keep you both focused in building and maintaining a healthy relationship.

8) Don't neglect the spiritual dimension of healing. One of the advantages those of faith have is ways to deal with the moral and ethical guilt created by an affair. Often disciplines and perspectives can help a person not only deal with the guilt of what he's done, but the spiritual attitudes and practices that will aid in the healing process.

My wife, being a Christian, acknowledged her growing distance from God leading up to the affairs. She mentioned how she kept God in a closet much of the time during her affairs, and how hard it was to approach Him after it was all discovered. Then, as she emerged from the fog and faced the reality of what she'd done to me and herself, the immense guilt overtook her for months.

During all this time, our priest was instrumental in her spiritual recovery. This was key because it directly influenced her recovery in all other areas of the marriage. It also allayed one of my big fears upon discovering her sin, that we'd spend eternity apart from each other if she didn't change course. Key also is the fact that seeing her struggle spiritually enabled me to see she was working on all parts of her life, not just emotional or practical boundaries, but making herself stronger spiritually, which reinforced in me the sense that she was doing all she could to fix herself.

If you are or have held a faith, this is the key time to bring yourself back to that faith for support and strength and help in dealing with all the hard issues you have to face. You need to hear from God, "Neither do I condemn you. Go and sin no more," just as the adulterous woman heard that from Jesus. You'll never hear that by avoiding God. Only by coming to Him in repentance and humility. But dealing with this can be a long road. There are many consequences to work through. As Scripture also says, the sin of adultery is, at its heart, a sin against your own body, your own self. Healing that will require spiritual aid as well as the other steps discussed above.

One practice I gave my wife was to memorize Psalm 51 and say it everyday. If you don't know, Psalm 51 is often referred to as the psalm of repentance. In the case of adultery, it is on target, because this is a psalm King David wrote upon being convicted of not only committing adultery with another man's wife, but having him killed so he could have the man's wife for himself. I knew she would need the constant reminder not only that she could repent and be forgiven by God and me for what she'd done, but the humble attitude needed to rest in God's forgiveness. It became one of the spiritual crutches that helped her through the months when the guilt weighted heavily on her soul as she worked to accept His forgiveness.

9) Work to fall out of love with the affair partner(s). If you felt you loved your affair partner, this is a hard one and will take many months to accomplish. But it is important for the following reasons.

One, the relationship was immoral and should have never started to begin with. It is important that the unfaithful spouse do all they can to erase the improper relationship from their lives. Your love for the affair partner is an affront to your spouse.

Two, no one can love two people and give 100% to only one. The love for the affair partner(s) is love stolen from your spouse who you pledged it to.

Three, as long as you remain in love with the affair partner(s), you are susceptible to temptation to reignite the fires of that relationship. Time alone will not kill off love. You can be ten years of no contact, and if the love never died, it can fire back up into another affair.

At first, it will be hard to do the following, but as you establish no contact successfully, and you gain some distance from the affair, you'll want to make sure you do the following.

One, make sure no contact is fully established, including getting rid of any items or messages or pictures associated with the affair partner. These items serve as remembrances, and provide a link to keep the flame alive.

Two, as you emerge from the fog induced by infatuation, make a list of all the negative things you ignored about the affair partner. In Lenita's case, he had more of an anger problem than I do. I'm very emotionally stable, and she is highly sensitive to anyone being angry to her. He would have, at some point, crushed her love and self-esteem. But in the midst of the affair, she didn't think about it and he remained on his best behavior.

Three, practice guarding your thoughts using distraction and other techniques as described in the "Healing Steps for the Hurt Spouse" chapter. You can't so easily stop thoughts of them from popping into your mind, but you can work to not dwell on them. They slip out as soon as they arrive. The less you think about them, the faster you fall out of love with him.

Four, focus and work on loving your spouse as fully as you can using the resources mentioned in the "read books" step. Investing yourself into loving your spouse will not only regenerate feelings of love for him, but also make feelings you had for your affair partner pale in comparison.

There are many other details we could go into, but the books listed will have more of that than we could ever hope to squeeze into one chapter. But the above are the core issues to deal with to help your hurt spouse heal and save your marriage. It is a lot of work and will take a long time, but the reward can be very worth it both in terms of your own healing and growth as a person, as well as a fuller and richer marriage, despite the negative affects of the affair.

Should I Tell?

In the book, "After the Affair," the author lists several reasons why an unfaithful spouse might not want to confess the affair to their spouse, and some reasons for doing so. I found the section on why to continue hiding the affair to be shortsighted because he missed a key reason that trumps most reasons to hide the information. I can understand an unfaithful spouse might list them as reasons, but in the overall scheme, they don't justify not telling.

First, let's take a look at some valid reasons why you may not want to tell your spouse about an affair. I can only think of two general categories.

One, if married to an abusive spouse who will likely harm you, then it may not be safe to tell. Rather, the first order of business is to get out of that relationship. Someone who has abused you is not a husband. Paul admonished that a husband must be willing to die for their wife, as Christ died for the Church. To abuse you instead is a form of emotional adultery and a tearing apart of the marriage. As long as there is a physical or emotional threat to you or any children, you have a responsibility to extract yourself from that situation. Call your county's or state's women's shelter, usually listed in the local phone book.

That said, his abuse didn't give you an ethical right to cheat on him. However, due to the potential for further hurt and the mind-control games an abusive spouse will use, it would not be wise to tell him about any affairs that have happened. The destruction of the affairs on the marriage takes a back seat to emotional and physical abuse and the need for you to get out of that relationship as soon as possible.

Two, if the relationship is breaking apart, a divorce is the likely outcome in the near future, and there is little hope to rebuilding, there is not much reason to tell. The main reason to tell is to heal the relationship. If either one or the other of you have lost hope that you could ever reach that place, or have lost all desire to try, there isn't much of a reason to confess the affair. But the moment that changes, the moment you both realize you want to see if the marriage can be saved, this reason no longer applies.

In short, any marital situation where hope is lost and the only real solution left, because of circumstances, is to part ways, means either there are bigger fish to fry before you even get to worrying about healing the devastation from an affair, or because of that, there is no purpose in telling since there is no hope in healing the relationship. So we could probably think up a few more examples, if we worked at it, where telling wouldn't be in anyone's best interest. But the key difference on that front is whether there is any intention of rebuilding the marriage or saving it.

There are other reasons often given by an unfaithful spouse as to why they don't want to tell. Let's take a look at some of them.

It would only hurt the spouse to know. Indeed, I've heard some spouses say they wish that they hadn't found out. They would have been happier in ignorant bliss, thinking their marriage was perfect even though it was not. But that's the problem with either spouse on that front. No matter whether the hurt spouse knows it or not, they have been hurt, they have been betrayed. Even if they are blissfully unaware of it, it will damage the marriage and poison the relationship. The only difference is the hurt spouse will be scratching their head why their spouse is growing distant and cold to them. The hurt spouse was hurt when the affair happened, not when they discover it.

In our online support forums, we are members both of the "Infidelity" support group and "Cheaters Anonymous." In both groups the question has been asked, "Should I tell?" While in the CA forum, most will say not to tell, in the Infidelity forum, well over 98% of the hurt spouses will say they should tell, that they would want to know, despite the hurt, rather than to live a lie. Bottom line, the hurt spouses generally want to know, are willing to be hurt to know the truth. A desire to not hurt them, therefore, shouldn't factor into whether to tell. They want to know even though it is painful.

I've heard some unfaithful spouses say it would be selfish of them to tell and hurt their spouse. The above makes it clear it is selfish to not tell, as the hurt spouse has a right to know. The real reason the unfaithful spouse doesn't want to tell isn't because it will hurt their spouse (that has already happened when you had the affair), but because you don't want to face their hurt and experience their hurt. That is selfish.

It was only sex, no emotional attachment. "I didn't love her. I only had to fill a need my spouse wasn't supplying, so what is wrong with that? She wouldn't understand." There are a lot of varied reasons that can be rolled into those justifications. It boils down to the feeling that the unfaithful spouse has convinced themselves that they were justified in seeking out what their spouse either wouldn't or couldn't provide them, whether sex, respect, a feeling of excitement, an ego boast, etc. So they feel there is no reason to tell the spouse because it really meant nothing in relation to their marriage. It is perceived to be no different than if you had needed some toilet paper, so you go get it yourself without telling your spouse you did so, and feel no need to "confess" spending money on that.

But such an approach denies the real damage that has been done. They are just that, justifications. An attempt to turn what you know was wrong into an innocent, even good thing. So why tell your wife just to see them suffer needlessly over it? At least, that's the reasoning.

It was a slip up, it's over, and I'll never do it again. Why bring it up and forever alter our relationship? This again is ignoring the damage. The relationship has already been altered greatly. Even if you don't perceive it now, the foundation of the way you interact with him has shifted. There is no doubt he has noticed this, but has written it off as an oddity or a phase you are going through unless he knows you've cheated before. Then his radar tends to be at a higher level of awareness.

Our marriage might end if I tell. Well, yes it very well might. After all, an affair tends to be taken as a rejection of the hurt spouse. Whether it was intended by you to be that or not, filling a "deficiency" you saw in your spouse or marriage, it is the stealing from the spouse by giving what is not yours to give to another person. It is a betrayal. There are spouses that are not able to get past that fact. That's the very real risk a person takes when they decide to cheat.

Yes, decide. I know some feel they fell into it, didn't have control, got drunk, etc. But you knew when you were crossing boundaries that were likely to lead to that destination. If a river is flooding and there is swiftly flowing water, you don't go wading in the shallows. By deciding to wade in the shallows where it is "safe," you subject yourself to the swift moving waters that can carry you away. You decided to flirt with that woman or man. You decided to go with him or her to get a drink at the bar when you know you do stupid stuff when drunk. You decided a dinner date with your boss was innocent and "just business" even though you've felt the chemistry between you.

It is the hurt spouse's call as to whether they continue the marriage or not. They are the one's who have been violated, who have been hurt by the betrayal. They have a right to know about it and decide what direction to take, how and if they can incorporate that reality into their future. You made your decision, it is wrong to deny them the chance to make theirs as well, just because you fear it will not be what you want.

The above reasons have a couple of things in common. One, they all assume the unfaithful spouse wants to keep the marriage, and so one reason he doesn't tell is to avoid an angry spouse walking out on him, and two, they are avoidance of dealing with the issues. It is a hard thing to come to your spouse and tell them something you know is going to shake their world. It is hard to sit before them and destroy their respect for you. It is much easier to avoid facing those demons, stay silent, and hope it will all go away.

If you want to keep the marriage, hiding this secret will increase the odds your marriage will end, not reduce it. For two big reasons. One, if he finds out about the affair on his own, his respect and trust in you will be more damaged than if you'd come clean. At least if you approach the subject with him, and confess, he'll know right from the start that you're being honest with him. If he had to discover it and drag it out of you, automatically you'll have a much deeper hole to climb out of from the beginning. Honesty will get you a lot of points and a much better chance of succeeding at rebuilding than lies, living a secret life, and hiding what you've done to him. Yes, he will still have a hard time dealing with it and will be angry, disillusioned, depressed, the whole nine yards. Trust in you will be damaged, but at least the damage will be less because you willingly came forth to tell him.

Two, the other big reason is if you don't tell, the chances of the issues that led to the affair being addressed and fixed in you are greatly reduced. Which even though you may have made a pact with yourself to never do that again, means you are likely to repeat the act, and even develop an addiction the longer it continues. The need to keep something secret is like someone blackmailing you. It causes you to go to great lengths to keep the secret hidden. It becomes a denial tactic, so you don't have to face the pain of what you did. It is these hidden, festering secrets that damage the marriage, create the cycle of shame since the guilt is never dealt with, and perpetuate the repeated cheating.

True, not everyone will repeat who doesn't tell. But it still means you don't deal with the reasons why you cheated, and that can be manifested in your relationship in other ways than cheating. It will result in not addressing the marital issues that perhaps strengthened the temptation, and so are still there to cause the same struggle again. Even if you never cheat again, the damage it caused you and the marriage will remain broken, and will only get worse with time, not better.

Someone I knew had a MRSA infection on their foot. It ate a good deep hole into his foot before the infection was stopped. One of the task that had to be done, almost daily in the beginning, was to remove the previous gauze and pack in fresh gauze. Based on his report, this was an exceedingly painful process. He likened it to being worse than passing a stone. Yet if he wanted it to heal, he had to do this painful process daily for a while. As it healed, it became less painful and had to be done less frequently. If not done, the infection could have returned and he could lose his foot, even die if it got into his blood stream.

The same type of situation results when there is unfaithfulness in a marriage. It creates an infection, and the only way to deal with it is through a painful process, mostly involving the unfaithful partner, but certainly the hurt partner also facing the reality of what has happened. If that painful process is shortchanged, so too will be the healing, and the infection will continue and grow bigger until it severely damages the relationship or causes it to die.

So what is the big reason why you should tell that trumps all these other reasons? It is because of this one, simple, but definitive fact: there will be no healing of yourself or the marriage until this is brought out in the open and dealt with by both spouses. Why?

Primarily for the reasons we've just been talking about. Keeping this secret hidden hurts the marriage and makes it more likely, not less, that the marriage will end in a bad way, or at a minimum, negatively affect your marriage and family for as long as you remain together. But why does it do that?

Pure and simple, there is no motivation to change until it is brought into the light. If you and your spouse do not change things, the infection that brought about the cheating will continue to destroy your marriage and relationship. If not in another affair after you had promised yourself you'd never do it again, the infection will come out in other ways. Like a coldness to the spouse, shame will cause you a lack of confidence in bed, or in dealing with the kids, or it will come out in anger and being overly critical with the spouse to compensate for your own shortcomings, and any problems with the marriage before the affairs will now loom as unbearable. You'll likely maintain positive thoughts about the affair partner, stealing part of your heart from your spouse.

But once you watch your spouse crumble under the knowledge of what you've done, suddenly the abstract, theoretical justifications that this wouldn't hurt anything are tossed out the window. Once you come face to face with the effects of your own actions, you'll face the full guilt, that until then, had been hiding in the shadows of your heart. Once you see and experience the devastation on the spouse and marriage, then, and only then, will you have the desire and motivation to fix what allowed you to do this to yourself, your spouse, your family, and your marriage. Your love for him, if there really is some there, will demand you do everything in your power to fix this. Why? Because when you face the full force of what you've done, only then are you freed to do the things that will bring about healing.

But what do many unfaithful partners do when they are discovered? They do their best to sweep things under the rug in order to avoid facing the guilt, to avoid facing their hurtful actions. They refuse to talk about it. They shift the blame for the affair onto the faults of the hurt spouse. They justify their actions. They downplay the damage done to the spouse. They expect the spouse to "just get over it" in short order. Essentially they hide from their responsibility and their ownership of what happened. Because of that, the issues that need to be dealt with to heal the marriage don't get fixed, and later it all explodes after a year or two of trying to "get past it."

That is exactly why not telling your spouse will cause your marriage to fail. Because keeping it a secret is nothing more than the most extreme form of sweeping it all under the rug. Out of sight, out of mind equals out of solutions and out of healing. If the goal is to keep the marriage, then only when the affairs are brought to light and both parties can work through them as a team, will there be any expectation of a happy marriage, or a marriage at all. If you keep them hidden, you doom yourself and your spouse to a joyless marriage at best and a shredded marriage at worst.

The best analogy I can come up with is getting cancer. My sister-in-law came down with cancer several years ago, and fought it for around four or five years before it took her life. In the midst of that fight, her husband grew gravely ill. When her sister visited, she said he looked like he was dying. She forced him to go to a hospital. The diagnosis? He had cancer, and they gave him less than a week to live. He died three days later. He had ignored the pain, the symptoms, the warning signs, because he didn't want to face the reality of what was happening to him. He didn't want to "hurt" his wife already struggling with her own cancer. He left a wife who had only a couple years to live and a daughter who now would be without a father and mother all because he didn't want to "tell" the pain he felt.

Once the affair has happened, it is the equivalent of marital cancer. Once the marriage has contracted it, the sooner the patient realizes and confesses he or she has it, no matter how painful it is to discover that, the sooner healing can take place. The easier it will be for healing to happen. The higher the success rate of saving the marriage from the disease. But refuse to admit it is there, and suddenly you wake up to a marriage that is nearly dead, and there is nothing that can save it. Not telling prevents healing.

Which is why most reasons given by unfaithful partners as to why they don't want to tell are nothing more than attempts to keep things hidden so they don't have to face the reality of what they've done. So they don't have to deal with the hard truths. So they can avoid fighting the demons that are busy eating away at their lives and marriage. Because telling and facing the music is not an easy thing to do. It takes guts and courage. It takes a real man or woman to admit they've screwed up, take full responsibility for it, own it, stare guilt in the face, and tell their spouse the truth. It takes a deep love for their spouse to confess so that you can begin to set things right and get the help you both need to not only heal the devastation of the affair, but to build a stronger marriage as well.

So you're ready to tell. How do you go about it? Here are some tips to take into consideration so it will go as smoothly as possible.

Tip One: don't tell him in a public location. It will not act as a restricting agent on the spouse's emotional reaction, and is more likely to cause both of you embarrassment when the spouse reacts with any extreme emotion, whether anger or crying. Instead, plan to do this in a private place, away from the public, away from the kids, in a safe place where the spouse can react naturally and honestly to what you are telling him.

But don't go to the opposite extreme and take the spouse to a hotel or other anniversary-like outing. You don't want to set him up as if you are going out to have a good time, only to hit him with the bad news. Rather pick a location that isn't associated with a vacation, anniversary, or other recreational place you like to visit. As tempting as it is because it is private, a vacation house, for instance, may be a bad idea. Keep in mind, your spouse is going to associate anything related to this event in his mind negatively from here on out. It will be a trigger. So the less you can make things like a particular location you like to go a trigger, the better.

One good idea is to take him for a drive in the country, if you don't normally do that. Simply tell him that you want to go for a drive. That you have some serious matters to discuss with him, and it is the best way to take some time to do it. Ideally, stop at a roadside table or lookout that is deserted so you aren't distracted by driving. There may be other ideas. But put some thought into it so you can avoid having a location be a trigger in the future.

Also, one of the advantages you'll have if you tell, is you'll be able to time it to help avoid triggers. Avoid telling close to specific days like Valentine's Day, Mother's Day, Thanksgiving or Christmas, birthdays, your anniversary, or any other important day in your family's tradition. Avoid telling a few days before such an event, but opt for several days after one instead. While these celebration days will seem empty and a hard time for the first year or two for the hurt spouse no matter the timing, having the discovery of the affair linked with a celebration will forever mar that celebration.

In my case, I discovered the affair four days before our 29th anniversary. From here on out, I will not be able to celebrate my anniversary with my wife without being reminded of the affair she had. It has not stopped us from healing, but it would have been better if I had found out on a generic day during the year that didn't hold any meaning for me. If you're telling, you'll have more control over the timing to help avoid celebrations becoming affair triggers.

Tip Two: plan ahead what you are going to say. You don't want to do this off the cuff, because if you do, you're likely to say the wrong thing and make it worse than you would have otherwise. Here are some ways to make this as good as it can possibly be told.

Plan on telling him in person. Not with a letter, an email, text message, or over the phone. You and he will need to see body language and facial expressions to avoid misunderstandings. It is simply the polite thing to do. Serious issues like this are not related other than in person if it can be helped.

Plan on starting by telling your spouse that you have something you hate to tell him, but that you have made some bad choices that have hurt him. In other words, start out owning up to your responsibility. Chose your words carefully to avoid, as best you can, anything that will sound like you are trying to minimize what you are about to tell him. For instance, you don't want to tell the spouse you've made a mistake. You may feel you did, that it was a case of poor judgment or just not thinking, but this will sound much bigger than a simple mistake to the hurt spouse. Such words will sound like you are trying to diminish that what you did was bad.

You want to communicate that you are at fault, that you are owning the responsibility for it. Be aware of this in the ensuing conversation. One of the first questions the hurt spouse will ask is "Why?" Be aware that nothing you can say will be an adequate answer. State that right up front. But avoid any explanation of why that sounds like you are shifting the blame onto the spouse or justifying your actions. None of that will be adequate, and the reasons why you did what you did will be investigated by you and your spouse in the days to come. So the only thing you really can say that doesn't sound like a justification or blaming on someone other than yourself, and still have a kernel of truth in it, is to simply say that you were tempted and you gave in.

So think ahead of time what likely questions your spouse will have, and what answers you'll give him that are both honest, but not sounding like you are attempting to shift blame from yourself. If you don't plan on what to say, you'll likely fall into sounding the wrong way to your spouse.

Tip Three: be sure to confess everything. You'll want to get everything out on the table so it can all be dealt with. The worst thing you could do, because you want to save face, is to only confess to the lesser events. If you did some online sex chats and had a physical affair with someone, don't confess to just the online sex chats. If you don't confess everything, the above reasons for confessing won't help you. You can hold back no secrets and hope to free yourself up to deal with them.

Also, you don't want to leave things for the hurt spouse to discover later. Nothing hurts trust and rebuilding more than to discover that your spouse has lied to you, hasn't told you everything. So you don't want anything left out there, no surprise secrets they can discover that will cause all the work you are going to be doing to fall apart in a matter of seconds. If you're going to confess so you can deal with it, then there is no reason to hold anything back. Get it all out in one shot. Then everything will be in the light and you can start the rebuilding, if the spouse is willing, without worrying that it will all be for nothing if he finds out this other secret.

Because of that, it is a good thing to go over the time line of the affair. The hurt spouse will want to know a general outline of what happened, and when. He doesn't need details, like how and what positions. If they demand to know that, after warning them it may not be productive for their healing, let them have that information. But he'll want to know when it started, what the conditions were when it started, what happened, how long did it last, whether it ever became a physical affair or remained emotional, or whether it was purely physical with little to no feelings of love involved. How you ignored the consequences you knew would result from it, how you hid it from them, where you both went, what you did together, how many times did you have sex, did you use protection, etc. If you go through the time line ahead of time and write down any relevant information, you won't accidentally skip something important that they will later say, "What? You never told me about her!" Any attempt to say, "Sorry, I forgot," will sound like a cop-out whether true or not.

Tip Four: remain as business-like as possible. I don't mean refuse to show any regret or remorse. That will likely come through anyway. But any dramatic emotional displays, like excessive crying or grief, will look more like an attempt to gain sympathy than a confession of guilt. What I mean is, stick to the facts and state the truth of the situation as plainly and clearly as you can.

For example, one good way to confess would be something along these lines: "Honey, I've done something horrible to you and the family. Three months ago, I was tempted by my own desires for another woman and I gave into them."

Then add on any more relevant detail. That is just an example. But you'll notice it is straight forward, doesn't beat around the bush, and is quick. Meanwhile, you are taking responsibility and that it was due to your own short comings, so there is no blameshifting or justification here. Say the bare facts, and then wait for the spouse to react and begin to ask questions.

Tip Five: Answer all questions as honestly and completely as you can, no matter how painful or difficult it is for you to face. These questions will go on for sometime. Don't expect them to stop after one good sit-down session. They will go on for months, maybe years. Until the hurt spouse feels he has as complete a picture as he can as to what happened and has come to terms with it. Don't hide anything here, as tempting as it may be.

Tip Six: read through the stages of grief chapter in this book. Your spouse will be experiencing a huge loss and will be working through these stages until he reaches acceptance. It will help you know what to expect and how to help him work through it if you know this information ahead of time. For instance, knowing that denial tends to be the first reaction, you'll know the impact of your confession won't sink in right away. He will be hoping it is a joke, or a Candid Camera skit. You're likely to hear the first words that come out of his mouth be, "No, no, no!" Knowing this, you won't be surprised when you get denial, anger, depression, as he works through dealing with this loss. Also, knowing this information will aid you in dealing with your own losses.

Tip Seven: promise you will work to never let this happen again, and then work on yourself like you mean it. Read books, go to counseling, spend time with your spouse, give him whatever he needs to heal, and let him see you as you really are. Open up your whole life to him and hide nothing. If you have trouble talking, aside from working on that with a counselor, use email, text, and letters to let your spouse know what is going on. Tell him everything, like any time you see the affair partner. You might think that will hurt him, but in truth, it builds trust because he knows you are not hiding what you could easily hide. Every time my wife sees her affair partner on the road or accidentally encounters him, she tells me about it. I don't even have to ask. It was a big indicator to me that she was being honest, because if she was still with him, the last thing she'd tell me is that she saw him that day.

Bottom line? Be as honest and forthcoming as you can. It is the only thing that will bring healing, and the only real chance you have to save your marriage and make it even better. While at first the hurt spouse will react with pain and crying and who knows what other emotions, if you are honest it will eventually come through as such. Don't expect to regain trust any time soon. It will take months, if not years. It will take no further secrets coming out down the road. It will take working on the marriage itself, to make it better and stronger.

Yes, you could lose the marriage if you tell. That is a definite possibility. I'm not going to suggest if you follow all this advice, you'll have a "happily ever after" outcome. But I do believe that telling in this manner will give you, your spouse, and the marriage the best chance for success that you can get, and for healing to happen. Not just to repair the damage, but to rebuild something new, something good and enjoyable, even in the midst of loss and a past life no longer possible to reclaim. If you don't tell, I can almost guarantee you'll find yourself in a deteriorating marriage and in more danger of a divorce in the end, than would have been true if you'd confessed to the affair.

Because a healthy marriage, whether it ever experiences an affair or not, is an honest marriage, where the spouse knows your faults and weaknesses, and loves you anyway. If you love your spouse, you'll not want any secrets to get in the way of a quality relationship with them.

Sexual Addiction

The following link is a set of "screening addiction tests" for men and women. A lot of times, people respond to an affair, mainly the unfaithful spouse, by feeling they had little to no control over themselves in the affair, conclude they have a sexual or related addiction. Often the unfaithful spouse tries to stop, but they can't seem to help themselves. But a clinical diagnosis of sexual addiction is much more involved than that. Just because you have felt that way, doesn't mean you are an addict. But it may mean you still need help overcoming the temptation so that it doesn't evolve into a true addiction.

To evaluate your risk, there are some helpful test you can find online, called "Sexual Addiction Screening Test (SAST)." http://www.sexualrecovery.com/resources/self-tests/gsast.php You can take that test to get a rough idea if there is reason for concern.

Whether one easily succumbs to temptation, or has become addicted to a certain sexual or related behavior, one must realize that he cannot get out of this on his own. They will need help. Accountability plays a big part in overcoming temptation. That is in part what Alcoholics Anonymous does for alcoholics. That takes some work and allowing someone else who can help into your private life. The more you keep it hidden, the less likely you'll be able to break out of it. You can't do this on your own.

A similar program to AA is SAA, Sex Addicts Anonymous. http://saa-recovery.org/ If the above test says there is some concern, that group would be a good place to start with. They can lead you to more resources than we could list here.

But don't jump the gun and assume you're an addict either. Treating it as an addiction may hide the real issues that are at the root of the cheating behaviors. Seeing a certified counselor in these areas can help you to arrive at the right conclusions and treatments for your specific situation. The above test can only identify risks.

But in any event, get help. The cycle can be broken.

Part 3 – For the Hurt Spouse

Should I Leave or Stay?

This is often one of the first questions a hurt spouse will ask themselves, and can return at later dates if rebuilding takes some hard hits. Do I rebuild the marriage or "cut my losses" and move on? Many hurt spouses will bounce back and forth between these options, unsure which way to go. Surprisingly, what I've frequently heard is a hurt spouse will say, before discovering the affair, that if he found that his spouse was cheating, the marriage would be over. But after finding out, his tune changes.

There are actually a lot of variables as to whether one might decide to leave or not, and many of them are subjective. So it is difficult for an author on this side of the book to tell you what is best in your situation. What I can do is give you some concepts to think about so you can arrive at your own decision.

First, keep in mind you don't need to be in a hurry to divorce. Shirley Glass in *Not Just Friends* recommends waiting at least three months after discovering an affair before making any "life-changing" decisions. Others have suggested waiting six months.

Point being, the weeks right after discovering an affair are so emotionally charged, it will be difficult to evaluate what directions to head. It is usually smart to allow the emotional roller coaster to slow down before trying to hop out of the cart.

But the truth is you are free to consider divorce if things don't work out, but you may never know if they will work out or not until you try. Once you start the divorce proceedings, your mind will tend to go into give-up mode, not committed-to-rebuild mode.

An exception to that advice is if you are in an emotionally and/or physically abusive relationship. I would highly recommend separating immediately, and potentially considering divorce unless they submit themselves to intensive therapy and treatment. Contact your local social services office to help you, but do whatever it takes to leave that situation, especially if you have children involved.

Second, I would encourage giving rebuilding a chance. This may be difficult. At first, your heart may not be in it. It may take you a while to get out of intensive care to move forward in healing. The unfaithful partner may not be cooperative, or either of you may start out sweeping issues under the rug to fester.

Within that first six month period, you'll get a feel whether your spouse and you can invest enough commitment to give rebuilding a chance. Some haven't seen any real growth or movement in the first year, and then things change. It can vary a lot depending on the circumstances and persons.

Third, if rebuilding isn't a viable option, start with separation. Some people won't change until it is evident you are headed out the door. Many unfaithful spouses think you won't leave, that there are not any serious consequences to fooling around other than your displeasure when they are caught. After three to six months of separation without any real change, perhaps you'll have your answer.

Fourth, if after doing all you can in the following chapters, and the unfaithful partner still isn't responsive to real rebuilding, it is healthier to let them loose than to keep them in the marriage. Sometimes the last resort we have for their awakening and return is to let them go.

Some Christians don't believe in divorce. I was one of them. I still don't think it is the ideal. But Jesus did say that due to the hardness of your hearts, Moses allowed a certificate of divorce to be given. He was acknowledging the fact that we live in a fallen world. If one's spouse is hard of heart and won't do the things to heal the marriage, it would be for his best interest to cut him off. Like the father released the prodigal son not because he wanted his son to waste his inheritance on wonton living, but in hopes of his ultimate redemption when he came to his senses, so one might divorce their spouse out of love for them, not hate.

Fifth, some hurt spouses stay because of financial reasons or the children. On the financial front, there are groups that can help. Check with your local social services office. You can also plan and prepare during your six month wait, in case. Get your financial ducks in a row, lay out your plan, meet with a lawyer to find out what to expect, etc. Then after six months or a year, if you have determined it just isn't going to work and you want out, you'll be ready.

With children, there will rarely be a good time. I would consider the home atmosphere. Are the children picking up that something is wrong? They can be more perceptive than you think. Such stress can be as much, if not more, of a problem for them than separating. If the marriage is miserable, the children will feel that and be insecure in the family. Some may even feel they must be doing something wrong that is causing the difficulty between you.

Six, you know your own marriage better than anyone. If your marriage was hanging on by a thread before learning of the affair, you may feel it is over on discovery day and want nothing more to do with him. Or you may not be ready to give up on your spouse even though everyone is telling you to. Everyone's "I've had enough" line is drawn in different places.

One member of our support group, known affectionately as "L", puts it this way: you'll know when you're done. Until then, keep working on rebuilding. If you have to ask yourself, "Should I leave?" Then you're not there yet.

The following chapters are to hopefully discover if rebuilding is possible for you. If after giving the following steps a try, you find yourself saying, "I'm done," then at least you know you gave the marriage the best chance to heal and can walk away knowing you did all you could do to salvage the relationship.

Healing Steps for the Hurt Spouse - General

While true that the unfaithful spouse carries the bulk of the work to rebuild from an affair, what types of things aid a hurt spouse in this? It is tempting to sit back and think the hurt spouse doesn't need to do anything to help heal from the hurt, that it is the unfaithful spouse who needs to change and fix everything. But this is not true. If rebuilding is to work, both spouses need to invest in the rebuilding 100%, or it will likely fail. That means the hurt spouse also has to be on board with making the necessary changes. In this section for the hurt spouse, we'll examine the actions and principles that the hurt spouse needs to heal from the affair.

I need to add some disclaimers before we start. One, everyone's situation is different. I will be, of necessity, speaking in more general terms. But something here may not apply to certain situations, or I may not list something that is needed in others. So take these as guides to check and make sure you are doing the things that will benefit you and your rebuilding efforts the most. Not as hard and fast rules to follow. Adapt, adjust, or throw out as needed.

Two, I've broken this up into three areas. A general area, when your unfaithful spouse is responsive and cooperating, and when he is not. The approach between the two are different, and when an unfaithful spouse becomes responsive, it may require a shift in approach if you determine it is genuine. But you will have some unfaithful spouses that are also cooperative at first, but later shut down. Some cooperate in certain areas, but not others. So depending on the situation, you may need to apply one set at one time, another at another time, and sometimes, a mixture. This chapter will be the general steps most hurt spouses will need to take into consideration.

1) First, realize you are not at fault for your spouse's affair. Many times an unfaithful spouse will attempt to say you are, and no doubt in their mind that is how they justified their decision to give into temptation, but the truth of the situation is the following. Despite whatever issues they had with the marriage or with you, cheating doesn't fix any of them. It only complicates and destroys things further. Therefore, the decision to cheat is never a good response to marital problems. Because of that, it is never your fault, no matter how bad of a spouse you've been or how difficult the marriage has been. Take responsibility for your part in the problems of the marriage, but not for their decision to cheat.

2) Don't automatically assume you have been rejected, and that there is something wrong with you. It is natural to feel they chose the other person over you. Because obviously as far as actions, that appears to be the case. It is usually a source of confusion to the hurt spouse why, if the unfaithful spouse says they love them, they could do something like this. How could they risk the marriage, the family, your sexual health, etc., on a fling? On a secret lover?

But the bottom line is this: in most cases, the unfaithful spouse never says to themselves, "You know what? I don't like X and Y, so I'll just go find someone else to have sex with." It happens, but the majority of cases is the unfaithful spouse becomes vulnerable due to their personal issues and needs, and gives into temptation without thinking about the consequences. As a matter of fact, the mind that is being tempted in this way is not rational at all. If it were, the person wouldn't do what their desires are wanting.

This state of mind is called a "fog" for good reasons, because the unfaithful spouse can't see anything other than what he wants right now. Though somewhere buried in the back of his mind he know this will hurt the marriage and his spouse, the strong desires he has, which may be sexual desires, ego stroking, attention, companionship, or a mixture of those, the desire for meeting those perceived "survival" needs blinds him to taking a serious accounting of the potential consequences. The stronger that desire is, up to an addiction, the less the later consequences play into the decision.

What happens for many unfaithful spouses is they give in at a moment of temptation without thinking through the consequences. As a result, they often come away feeling the victim, that it just happened, and so they start looking for reasons why. Often the finger is pointed at the spouse because he didn't do X, Y, or Z. They often don't feel like they consciously made a decision to cheat. What they miss is failing to recognize the decisions that led to the temptation to cheat, like choosing to flirt, believing it to be "innocent fun."

Often he didn't intentionally reject you by having an affair. He was tempted and let it happen. He gave in to his desires. That is often why he doesn't bring up his desires and needs with the spouse, because he doesn't identify them that way. Not too many unfaithful spouses wake up one morning and think to themselves, "Wow, I really have a need for intimate conversation with my spouse. I could talk to them about it, explain how desperately I need this, and we could go to marriage counseling. Or I could have an affair. Hum...the affair sounds like the best option." Usually those needs are ignored or erupt in anger and fights instead of constructive cooperation, and the unfaithful spouse isn't always directly aware they have become more vulnerable to temptation because of them.

So even if the unfaithful spouse says things like, "She made me feel better than you ever did, that's why I cheated," don't give into the lie that he chose her or him over you. Chances are the unfaithful spouse is coming up with reasons because he is too deep in the fog to believe it is his fault and accept blame for it. People cheat because of their own character shortcomings, not being able to deal with their problems in constructive ways. It is more a rejection of who they are than you.

"But she said she loved him, and she can't stop thinking about him." Yes, that happens. Unfaithful spouses all the time mistake infatuation for true love. They often get in it so deep they have a hard time realizing what they feel isn't love, but a feeling they enjoy and desire. Wearing the rose-colored glasses of infatuation, their love for their spouse will seem to pale in comparison on the passion level. But that isn't the fullness of love, and it cannot compete with real, unconditional love for each other if your relationship is based on more than passion and friendship, but a self-sacrificing love for each other.

In short, what he is often in love with isn't the affair partner, but in how the affair partner made him feel. He is in love with a feeling.

3) Realize that the healing process and rebuilding trust will take time. Two years minimum, maybe longer if the unfaithful spouse isn't fully cooperative, or you have trouble getting past issues. During that time, you'll have periods when you're making progress, and periods when it feels you've sunk back to day one. Even the best of rebuildings will experience periods of depression and a sense of loss on a recurring basis. Don't expect even two or three years down the road to be "past this." As time goes buy, assuming you both are dealing with the issues instead of shoving them under a rug, incidences of feeling the loss and the hurt will become less and less, duller and duller. But that takes at least two years or more, about the amount of time it takes for a couple to feel the changes in their life have become the "new normal." Even if the rebuilding goes well, don't expect the pain and hurt to be totally gone even at two years.

4) Know the stages of grief so you can work through each

stage, avoid getting stuck, and find acceptance. You can read up on them in Part 4 of this book. Realize that these emotions and struggles are normal and needed to heal, as painful as they are. Bottling them up and ignoring them can prevent healing.

5) Work toward a healthy and strong sense of self. Affairs can be big blows to one's self-esteem and sense of knowing who you are. The affair changes the relationship significantly from what it was before. Both in how you look at your spouse, but also in how you perceive yourself through your spouse's eyes. It will never be what it was prior to the affair.

Get individual counseling, read good books, and keep the following in mind. While you may have blame for some marriage problems, you are not to blame for the affair. That is fully owned by the unfaithful spouse and his affair partner. The reason they cheated, no matter what he claims the reasons were, are due to his inappropriate responses to issues he is facing within himself. There is a character flaw in him that allowed, maybe even sought out, the affair as the way to deal with his needs. It is not a lack in you, it is a lack in him that is the problem.

Therefore, to get your view of your self through him is going to be a very distorted picture. Don't rely upon it. Assume his view of you will be filled with distortions and exaggerations. He has proven himself untrustworthy in hiding the affair from you, he will be untrustworthy in other areas until he takes ownership of his wrongs and gets out of the fog enough to think clearly.

6) For those of faith, seek out spiritual counseling from your pastor/priest, or spiritual leader, or even a close friend who you feel is strong in the faith. While generally this is a tragedy not readily shared, especially among church members, and there can be some shame felt even by the hurt spouse for the fact it happened to them, you will need someone who is not emotionally impacted by the affair to keep your feet on solid ground.

For those of faith, this can be a time of faith crisis. Why did God allow this to happen? Why did my prayers for him not get answered? Approached the wrong way, some could lose their faith in God over this. Or, they will find their faith a firm foundation in the midst of the raging sea of emotions, hurt, and struggles to rebuild. Having someone that can give input and guidance to what you are going through can make the difference between healing and letting the pain crush you. If nothing else, you need a listening ear. You don't want to carry this struggle alone. Also your spiritual life is just as important, if not more so, than your emotional life, because it will impact your emotional life and can be the difference between a successful rebuilding or ending in divorce.

A disclaimer. Not all pastors or priest are adequately trained in dealing with affairs. Don't expect them to be marriage counselors unless they have a degree or certification in that area. But hopefully they can provide spiritual guidance. Some have unhelpful ideas about marriage and affairs based on their interpretation of the Bible. If one pastor or priest isn't helping you, seek out another who can. Some communions have more resources to deal with these things, or the pastor will know good counselors you can contact.

7) For successful rebuilding, you will want to eventually reach a stage of empathy with the unfaithful spouse. This won't happen quickly, certainly not right away. You are going to be too focused on your own pain, and your anger at what they did won't allow much empathy to take place. But in due time, as you work through the stages of grief, and if rebuilding is going to be successful, eventually you'll need to get there.

Notice, I did not say sympathy for them. Two different things. Sympathy is "feelings of pity and sorrow for someone else's misfortune." Empathy is "the ability to understand and share the feelings of another." Sympathy says you have pity on them and feel sorry for them. Empathy says you understand that their pain exists, even if you can't care about it or deal with it adequately right now. Empathy acknowledges that the other person has real needs, concerns, and difficulties in this journey as well. But for the hurt spouse to move past an obsession and focus on self and their own pain, they have to reach a place where they are able to understand the pain the unfaithful spouse is going through.

I'm not talking here about understanding the why or reasons for the affair. I'm talking about his hurts and pains. Believe me, he has them. Some of them are good at covering them up, even from themselves, and not focusing on them or dealing with them. While some unfaithful spouses are good at fooling themselves so that they seem to be immune to sorrow and repentance, they are just as damaged by the affair as their hurt spouse is. In some cases, even more so.

He has to deal with the reality that he committed an act against the one they love (if that's the case) and who he doesn't want to lose. He has been spiritually and emotionally damaged by living in the fog. As the Scriptures say, unlike other sins, fornication and adultery are sins against one's own body and person. He may try to cover up that pain by blame-shifting, gas-lighting, sweeping it under a rug and refusing to talk about it any longer, sticking his head in the sand by keeping busy, etc. to avoid facing up to it, but it is there.

He also has the initial pain, if the affair was ongoing when discovered, of breaking off a relationship he was enjoying, usually before he was ready to do so. One of the hardest things for the unfaithful spouse to do is break that relationship whether or not he felt he was "in love." Think back to an early relationship that broke up of your own, and how emotionally devastated you were.

Except here, there is the added hurdle to overcome, that he shouldn't talk about it or show those feelings to the hurt spouse because it further hurts them. So many unfaithful spouses struggle through that alone. Many cases, it leads them to reconnect with the affair partner. But the unfaithful spouse who successfully breaks that contact will experience a major loss. Though that is not what the hurt spouse wants to hear, that's the reality of the situation. He could no easier not feel that loss than if they had lost one of their parents to a car accident. It is one of the many negative consequences for being unfaithful.

For the unfaithful spouse who really puts forth the effort to fix themselves, he must endure the painful and slow process of facing his sins and misdeeds, owning them, staring their guilt in the eyes, repenting, and working on himself to ensure the sin doesn't happen again. Rebuilding for the unfaithful spouse is a painful process if he really invest himself in it. It too will take years, not weeks or months, before it is conquered. He will always live with the reality that he did this to the one he loves, and face her everyday with that knowledge.

Until you reach a stage of empathy for the unfaithful spouse, until you can find the ability to care for what they are going through, rebuilding will not happen. For what you are rebuilding to isn't just an existence with each other, but a rekindling of the love you have for each other. Without empathy, that will never happen.

8) Don't obsess over the affair partner. I know, it is natural to do so. Most hurt spouses at one point or another expresses anger over the other person who their spouses cheated with. They are convenient targets of hate, because you are not trying to rebuild with him. To express that blame and hatred to the spouse would be counter productive to the rebuilding. Also sometimes unfaithful spouses will not tell the truth about their affair partner, to deflect blame from themselves. "But Honey, she seduced me when I was depressed."

So often hurt spouses will want to meet the affair partner and tell them what for, or punch them, or destroy their property and lives.

But this will not be productive. It will only destroy you and keep you from healing, and take your focus off where it needs to be: on your spouse.

The only concern you should have about the affair partner is to make sure your spouse has broken all contact with him and then treat him as if that person doesn't exist. The affair partner become invisible. The goal should be to get him out of your lives as cleanly, quickly, and as forcefully as possible. The more you stir things up with him, the more likely he is to reestablish contact with your unfaithful spouse and stay in the picture, and continue to seek after what he once had. Because the only way the unfaithful spouse can break the bond he has with the affair partner is to go for a long time with no contact. The more contact he has, the less likely he'll break that bond, and the more likely he'll return to the affair partner.

9) Guard your thoughts. This is something that is learned. Many hurt spouses have instances of flashbacks, can't get the picture of their spouse in bed with the affair partner out of their head, imagine all sorts of scenarios that probably never happened between the two, usually blown out of proportion. But these thoughts tend to be obsessive. They intrude into your daily life, sex life, and when something triggers your memories of the affair. At first, these will be strong and need to be faced. But at some point, they become obsessive and can prevent the hurt spouse from healing. To do that, the hurt spouse (and the unfaithful spouse for other reasons) needs to learn the art of guarding your thoughts.

One method is to use distraction. One simple way is to have a phrase you say to yourself when those thoughts arise. For the more religiously inclined, a simple one to remember is what is known in ancient Christianity as the "Jesus prayer." The simple form is, "Lord have mercy," which is a response in prayers at many churches. The fuller form of it is "Lord Jesus Christ, Son of God, have mercy on me, a sinner." But even if you are not religious, you can find a phrase that can help distract you. A saying like, "Que sara, sara." That is, "Whatever will be, will be."

A second form of distraction is music or talk radio. Get your mind engaged in a song or discussion so it won't wander to the wrong thoughts. Strike up a conversation with someone. Give someone a call.

Another form of distraction is to do something physical. Many use exercise of some form. But that alone may not occupy your mind, though it can help burn off some steam. My wife was instructed to use a rubber band around her wrist, and when thoughts she didn't need to be thinking of arose, to snap it so that the pain would distract her from her thoughts.

Another method is reclaiming. This is especially good for triggers. If there is something that tends to make you think of the affair and other obsessive thoughts, reclaim that event. For example, my wife met her primary affair partner at the local gym. I didn't go, obviously, or it wouldn't have happened. Once I discovered the affair, I had two options. I could forbid her to go to the gym any longer, for fear she'd met him there again and this would keep going, or I could start going there myself to ensure he and no one else would hit on her. I opted for the later, in part because I didn't want remembrances of the gym to be her private domain of good thoughts about the affair partner, and I wanted to claim that joy they shared for me and her. So I went. Yes, the first time or three were awkward. But now I don't ever think anything about it. Driving by the gym holds pleasant memories of us working out and swimming together instead of remembrances of "this is where they started their affair, worked out together, swam together." Seeing the gym isn't a trigger to the affair as it would have been had I taken the other route.

A third method is to substitute positive thoughts for the negative. When the obsessive thoughts arise, have ready some positive thoughts to direct your mind to. If, for instance, images of your spouse in the arms of the affair partner arise during sex, causing you to lose all interest, have ready images of you and your spouse to shove in front of them.

All these things take some practice. At first you'll forget and suddenly remember, "Oh, I'm not supposed to be thinking on these things," and you'll do one of the things above. At first, it will have to be a conscious decision. But after a few weeks of doing these, they'll start to become automatic and natural. What you are doing is retraining your mind to not go there. In the first weeks after discovery day, forget it. You can't avoid thinking about it day and night, all the time. But as you move on, and some of those thoughts won't leave, you have to work to get them out and learn how to guard your thoughts so you control them, and not them, you.

10) Interact with the unfaithful spouse in a straightforward, clear, and business-like manner. Yes, at first your emotions are going to be running wild. Everyone's does. You'll probably say things that you later wish you could take back. But once you settle down from the initial roller coaster ride, you'll want to accomplish the following things in communicating with your unfaithful spouse.

First, what your goals and expectations of him will be. Include as short but complete of a list as possible. Transparency and what that practically means. Financial. Availability to answer your questions, and maybe an agreed upon method to do that. That he will allow you to vent and relate your hurt without him becoming defensive or shutting down on you. Read books together like *Not Just Friends*. Go to marriage counseling, committing for two to three months at least. Communicate that rebuilding will take years, so he doesn't have the idea it will blow over in a month or two.

The above are examples, you may have more depending on the situation. But the important thing is to make it clear what he will need to do to meet your needs to heal from what he has done to you.

Second, list the consequences of these not happening. One thing you will need to do, despite beliefs in never divorcing, is to leave the divorce option on the table. For some unfaithful spouses, they have convinced themselves that you would never leave them, and it gives them motivation to just get through the initial fallout from the discovery before picking back up where they left off. For them to be shaken out of their fog thinking, they need to feel you could really leave them. But draw that line carefully. Make sure you are ready to do that should it go that far. Nothing worse than drawing a line in the sand, to back up and draw a new line when that one is crossed. Then the lines mean nothing.

So I would suggest breaking them down in stages as much as possible, both loosening up as he does better, and tightening down if he falters. So, for instance, maybe one consequence of either not being transparent and/or of breaking no contact is he is forced to hand in his smart phone and get an old fashion, no frills, basic phone with no texting ability. Or he allows spyware to be installed on his phone so you can fully monitor him. Then after a period of time has passed, say six months as an example, and he's been good, that gets taken off his phone or restored to being smart. Or you first take an extended trip to a relative, and if that doesn't reverse things, separate. If he falters again, divorce after a certain amount of time has passed without resolution. Break it down into progressively more restrictive stages as required, and back them down as he becomes more cooperative.

Third, write down something similar for yourself, dependent on him or her doing the above. Be transparent yourself. Good marriages are transparent without an affair. Maybe you'll wash his clothes and fix his dinner. Find out what his needs are and seek to meet them. Don't assume they are the same as yours, because they won't be in most cases. Certain ones can be taken away if he isn't cooperative. Not to be manipulative, but to reward behavior that will help rebuild, and discourage behavior that will end in divorce court. The idea is you are joining him to work on this together, not just him doing all the work.

The idea is to have good communication. Don't rely upon hints and "he should know what I want" type ideas. Be clear about your needs and wants. He can't be expected to meet them or change for them if you don't voice them clearly. The communication needs to happen in a calm, rational manner. Not threats, ultimatums, and screaming. You also need to be firm and confident. A no-nonsense manner of "this is the way it needs to be if we're to make it. Are you with me or not?" Also allow the unfaithful spouse to communicate clearly to you as well. Make it a discussion, not a lecture. Not all of your goals need to be given at one time. You may start with a basic list, but add to it over time as new things pop up. Think in terms of short-term needs and where you want the relationship to be over time.

11) Get help through counseling and good books. Too many spouses have a lone-ranger attitude. I know, because that was me. Until Lenita's infidelity, I'd never been to a counselor for anything. Despite there were times we should have done so in the past. However, I knew this time I wanted to leave no stone unturned in our efforts to rebuild. I knew we had one good shot at healing. I knew we were in over our heads. We were treading new territory and needed a guide to avoid as many pitfalls as possible.

Since you are reading this book, it is likely you already have sensed the same thing. But perhaps someone shoved this book into your hands and you've reluctantly read it, though by this point you have no doubt discovered the value of this type of help or you would probably not still be reading by this point.

Books can be a major source of help in rebuilding both yourselves and your relationship. I'll recommended more books in the next chapter, but here I'd recommend the following book to begin your healing journey.

Getting Past the Affair: A Program to Help You Cope, Heal, and Move On -- Together or Apart by Douglas K. Snyder. The strength of this book is it gives you some practical steps to take in dealing with the affair, including the initial days and weeks after discovery day. It is based upon a sound understanding of the dynamics in rebuilding relationships, and can help if rebuilding doesn't succeed as expected or isn't the ultimate choice of either spouse. Also includes steps for the unfaithful spouse as well as the hurt one. For these reasons, I recommend reading this book first to get some immediate guidance and direction, including finer points on what we've talked about here.

While books like these and the one you are reading now are helpful, they can only be of a general help. The author(s) cannot cover every conceivable circumstance, nor address your specific situation. A person reading these books still needs to take the general principles and apply them to his relationship.

Because of this, it is also strongly suggested to obtain individual and marriage counseling as soon as possible. Both spouses need to evaluate how these events have affected them based on their history, how to rebuild their sense of self-identity, and what will be the best approach, given their specific circumstances, to proceed with rebuilding the marriage.

Once, I attempted to change the ball-joint on an AMC Pacer. I followed the instructions in a book, but a frozen bolt refused to come lose. It was then I read in the book, "This is not a 'backyard mechanic' type job." I thought, "Now they tell me!"

In the same way, rebuilding a marriage and yourself after an affair is not a do-it-yourself task. If you go it alone, chances of success go way down.

When you look for a therapist in your area, search for those with experience in helping with infidelity. Once attending sessions, if it is clear they are enabling rug-sweeping, blame-shifting, or other tactics which divert you from dealing with the issues, feel free to change counselors until you find one that can truly help you. Not all counselors are created equal, or in some cases, you just don't mesh well with a given counselor through no fault of either person.

These are some of the general steps. I could continue on and get more detailed, but this gives a broad overview of the general steps that can help a hurt spouse deal with the aftermath of an affair. Next we'll look at the steps a hurt spouse can take in dealing with a cooperative unfaithful spouse.

Healing Steps for the Hurt Spouse – Cooperative Unfaithful Spouse

The previous chapter looked at the general steps a hurt spouse needs to take for healing to occur. In this chapter, we want to take a closer look at the specific steps a hurt spouse can take toward healing with an unfaithful spouse who is cooperative.

First, what do I mean by cooperative? Does that mean he does everything he should do, right off the bat, perfectly? No, since few will ever do it perfectly, and the healing process is more a series of steps. By cooperative, I mean an unfaithful spouse who is actively working toward healing by consciously taking the steps to heal. Those steps are listed in the "Healing Steps for the Unfaithful Spouse" in Part 2. His attitude should be one of humility and repentance, rather than sweeping it under the rug and blame shifting. If he is willing to face the consequences of his actions and stick with it for however long it may take to help the hurt spouse heal, up to at least two years or more, and he takes the steps in progressive manner, he is cooperating.

As mentioned in the last chapter, an unfaithful spouse may start out cooperative but grow weary of the struggle and pain. It isn't easy. He may give up and withdraw at some point and become uncooperative. Likewise, an unfaithful spouse can start out uncooperative, but become cooperative as the affair loses its hold on him. Sometimes an otherwise cooperative unfaithful spouse on some issues will become uncooperative on others.

A warning is appropriate here. An unfaithful spouse can sometimes appear cooperative, but is doing it as a front to please you, to get you to settle down, but he is still either planning on getting back with the affair partner or is still secretly seeing the affair partner. All you have to go on is what you can see until you discover evidence to suggest he is putting on a front and being manipulative. You'll have to judge his attitude and decide which path to take. When he gets caught still headed down the wrong road, and you realize he hasn't been honest in their cooperation, then shift over to the uncooperative unfaithful spouse's path.

When it comes down to it, trust your gut. Maybe he appears cooperative on the outside, but the sixth-sense in your gut tells you something is not right. Get evidence before acting on it, but if your gut is sounding a warning, pay attention to it. Start investigating the warning. It will generally give you a good clue whether your spouse is being cooperative or not.

Also, an explanation about this path. It may seem to some that by doing some of these things, you are giving the unfaithful spouse a "free pass" and letting him off easy. But that is not the case. If your unfaithful spouse is responsive to rebuilding, the goal of these steps is to give the unfaithful spouse the best chance at succeeding. The rebuilding process for the unfaithful spouse is painful enough if he does it like he should. But if he doesn't respect the opportunity you are giving him and he violates it, then you move to the other list. But as long as he is doing what he needs to, the goal is to entice him to continue to do the right things, to work on rebuilding, and to stay honest with you about what is going on with him.

As mentioned in the previous chapter, the better he does, the more freedom he gets. If they blow it, then the restrictions get a little tighter to motivate him to straighten up, that this is serious, and you will not allow him to walk over you or your feelings. So keep in mind that these are steps with an unfaithful spouse who is cooperative. The steps change when they aren't.

Also, this is assuming that you have already laid out expectations and consequences as mentioned in the previous chapter. Here are the steps.

1) Think in terms of stages in healing. There are things you expect to happen pretty quick after discovery day. Most will list that the unfaithful spouse must become "transparent," which means he gives the hurt spouse the passwords and user names for all his accounts that are allowed to stay open, their email, social networking sites, and any cell phones and cell phone bills. Also, he is willing to discuss all aspects of the affair as needed. The unfaithful spouse has lost trust, and this is the only way to earn it back.

Also, the unfaithful spouse is expected to break all ties and contact with the affair partner pretty quickly. He is usually given a chance to tell the affair partner that the affair has been discovered and is cutting off all contact with her. But after that goodbye, nada. That is usually hard for the unfaithful spouse. From the hurt spouse's point of view, it is an illegitimate relationship that should have never happened in the first place, so the hurt spouse tends to not have much sympathy for the unfaithful spouse's struggles. But you can have empathy here as we discussed in the previous chapter, and know that because it isn't easy, most unfaithful spouses will have a period of time in coming to terms with this. Yet it is expected to happen fairly quickly after discovery day. The unfaithful spouse needs to understand that for the hurt spouse, until no contact is established, the affair is not over and no healing can happen.

But there are other things that the unfaithful spouse may hold onto at first, but need to change at some point. Whether the hurt spouse is willing to wait for those to happen would be spelled out in the expectations you've discussed with him. To avoid a lot of words to describe what I mean, I'll give an example from my experience.

Lenita had some pictures of both Clyde and Bubba. I told her early on that she needed to get rid of them, but she was reluctant. At that point, she still felt like she wanted to keep something to remember them by. I could have demanded she delete them and forced her to comply. But I also knew that doing so might push her to save some in a hidden place because she wasn't ready. Also, I had an ulterior motive for not pushing her. I wanted some things left to her decision so I could gauge whether she was making progress or not. I knew if she came to the place where she was ready to get rid of them, not only would she actually get rid of them all, but I would know she had arrived at a milestone. That didn't happen until around three months after discovery day.

As time went by, she dug deeper and made other changes that served to cut off remembrance of the affair partners that I couldn't have possibly known about or demanded so easily. She started guarding her thoughts, so when her thoughts turned to thinking about the affair partners, she took steps to distract herself and not focus on them.

It will mean more if your unfaithful spouse comes to some things on his own volition. Doesn't mean you don't express your desires on a point, as I did with Lenita, but I didn't press her to do it right then. If he is moving in the right directions, assume he'll get there, and it will confirm he is on the right course when he does it.

It is also important because you can only focus on so much at one time and implement it. Throw too many changes at someone too fast, and it can backfire. The more you can change together, cooperatively, the better.

As you evaluate things, decide what needs should be implemented immediately, and what types of changes you want the unfaithful spouse to make later when they are ready. If he is cooperative, then you are working together, so you want the minimum number of ultimatums possible. Only those things that have to happen to solve the immediate crisis of the affair trauma and to start the required healing should be required within the first weeks of discovering the affair. But if a certain item is causing you additional trauma, then communicate that a trigger is preventing you from healing. Be open and honest with the unfaithful spouse. You need to be transparent with him, just as he needs to be with you.

2) Praise successes. Make note of them. Highlight them. They will encourage you both to acknowledge progress. It is easy for the hurt spouse to allow negative emotions to overpower any and all positive movements forward. The hurt spouse will have a tendency to avoid praise for fear of seeming to act like the affair wasn't that bad. However, if an unfaithful spouse never receives acknowledgment for what he's done right, he can become disheartened over time and give up. Don't hand out false praise, but acknowledging his successes in rebuilding not only encourage him to keep moving forward, but encourage you as well.

3) Focus on healing the marriage as well as the affair. This one is critical. Sometimes, due to an uncooperative unfaithful spouse, healing the marriage gets put on the back burner. But with a cooperative unfaithful spouse, while not accepting that the affair was caused by marital problems, you will want to take this opportunity to deal with those issues. You have more motivation now to make major changes in the way you relate to each other in marriage than ever before.

Aside from the obvious benefit to the relationship itself, there is an affair related reason to focus on this when you have a cooperative unfaithful spouse. It significantly increases the chances of rebuilding succeeding. Willard F. Harley reports in his book, *His Needs, Her Needs: Building an Affair-Proof Marriage*, that in his practice of working with couples who have experienced infidelity, using the traditional methods of therapy, he had about a 40% success rate of them staying together, which is average. Some of those not happily staying together. But when he started focusing on helping them to rekindle the romantic fires in their relationships and working on the marriage itself, his success rate rose above 60%.

When you think about it logically, it makes sense. The stronger your marital bonds emotionally, spiritually, and physically are going into an affair, the more stability you have to weather the storms that an affair brings to the marriage. Marital problems may not be the cause of an affair, but focusing on them is part of the solution.

One of the key events that needs to happen for successful rebuilding is for the couple to "fall in love" again. Renew the fires of romance. Because there is no better healing for the hurt spouse than to feel his spouse is excited about him once again and wants him exclusively, and no better antidote to the unfaithful spouse yearning for the excitement of the affair partner and missing them than a burning love for his spouse. Several of the following suggestions will be toward that goal.

4) Spend around 15 hours a week together, minimum. Think about it. When you both first started your relationship, when you dated and became engaged, what did you do, primarily? One, you spent every bit of free time together, and two, you thought about each other all the time.

For the unfaithful spouse, this should be obvious, because that is exactly what he was doing with his affair partner. The reason that seemed so new and exciting was because he probably spent minimal time with his spouse, and when he did, it was often dealing with unpleasant things. "Honey, take out the trash. Honey, pay the bills. Honey, when is dinner going to be ready? Honey, do you have the money for Johnny's band trip?" Often the time is not spent gazing into each other's eyes over a romantic dinner, but dealing with the day to day stuff, and otherwise focused in your own worlds.

When you and he first met, naturally you focused on each other. You wanted to talk about your issues, thought the world of him and he of you, and he became the focus of your world. That was exciting. So what did you do? You spent as much time as possible with him. On the phone. Texting. In person. Emails. Facebook. Wherever you could fit it in. I can bet that you didn't talk about bills, trash, kids, or other such responsibilities for any length of time, if any.

"What are we going to do?" You'll need to figure that out, but in reality, it doesn't matter. If you can find an activity you both like, great. If not, let her pick one that the man will do with her, and the man pick one that she'll do. The point being, begin treating him as important, worth spending your time with. He should be the most important person in your life. How you spend your free time should reflect that priority. Then when the other person picks up that they are important to you, it will translate into the same excitement, and return that importance back to you.

What you'll find, whether it is just sitting at a Sonic sipping a coke, or working out together at the gym, or shopping together, or participating in a sport together, or having sex, is that it will engender those same romantic fires that originally got things rolling when you started dating. And please, don't focus mostly on the day to day stuff or once past the first month or two, on the affairs. Focus on your relationship, your future together, what you want to do, what your goals are, share your dreams.

At first, the affair will likely dominate your discussions, but at some point, you'll want to move beyond that. Bring up issues when needed, but remember, the goal is to rekindle romantic fires here and draw you both closer together, not always focusing on the hard and painful things. But if you spend that kind of time together, you'll find it easier to talk about the things that need talking about, and reestablishing the emotional bonds of marriage that will be a reward, making stronger bond to deal with the more painful parts of the rebuilding process.

5) Go to marriage counseling. If you want to discover from a more objective view where your marriage is weak, a great place to start is a marriage counselor in addition to seeing a counselor for individual help. They can help you spot weaknesses, and offer ways to improve them. The affair will likely play into it at first as far as issues to deal with, and the vulnerabilities in the marriage can highlight why the unfaithful spouse was tempted to allow an affair to happen. But it should move onto focusing on the marriage itself. The marriage counselor can also give you good books to read and other helps.

Going to a marriage counselor can also give opportunity to discuss some of the harder things in a more controlled environment. If communication often turns into fights and storming off, leaving the issues unresolved, a counselor can help to establish helpful patterns of conflict resolution that will enable you to talk to each other constructively rather than destructively.

A good idea is to commit to go to at least a month or two of weekly meetings. Too often, because one partner didn't like the initial visit or two, he doesn't want to keep going, especially if he is having trouble facing his responsibility for the affair. If a particular marriage counselor isn't really doing the job for you, find a different one. Don't use that as an excuse to not do it. But commit to giving it time to work.

6) Read some good books together. In addition to the book listed in the last chapter, here is an additional reading list you'll find helpful.

Not "Just Friends": Rebuilding Trust and Recovering Your Sanity After Infidelity by Shirley P. Glass. This book has a lot of good info on how to deal with the aftermath of an affair, but the strength of this classic treatment is assessing the motivations and experiences both hurt and unfaithful spouses go through. An excellent book for a couple to read together in evaluating each other's strengths and weaknesses in dealing with an affair, and what to do about them.

His Needs, Her Needs: Building an Affair-Proof Marriage by Willard F. Jr. Harley. You may not be ready for this book immediately after discovery day. You will probably need to wait until you have more emotional stability, until you're out of the emotional ICU. But the earlier you can read and process what is in this book, the quicker and smoother rebuilding will happen.

This book doesn't focus so much on dealing directly with the affair, but on expressing a passionate love to one's spouse in a way they can "hear" it, in order to heal the marriage. As mentioned earlier, this book had a profound impact on how Lenita and I interacted with one another. I learned what I had done that failed to tell her she was important to me, and how she failed to do the same to me. We both made some major adjustments, not just to fill the needs she unconsciously sought out during the affair because I wasn't doing so, but because I did love her but wasn't communicating that truth effectively for years. Instead, I'd often told her by my actions and decisions, "You're not that important to me." She did the same to me. This is no longer the case.

Without that sense of "he loves me and I'm important to him" communicated through actions, rebuilding is much less likely to succeed. It is the oil that provides the motivation to struggle through the painful process of rebuilding and offers hope that there is the reward of a happy future at the end. Ideally you'll want to read and discuss this book together.

How to Help Your Spouse Heal from Your Affair: A Compact Manual for the Unfaithful by Linda MacDonald. This book is the first book recommended for the unfaithful spouse to read because it will give him a fuller understanding of what the hurt spouse is dealing with, establish empathy, and the needed steps to help her heal, not to mention himself. I'm listing it here for the hurt spouse, however, because it is good to have a clear picture of what the unfaithful spouse should be doing. Not only to evaluate when your spouse is being cooperative or not, but also in evaluating what you are responsible for to make their efforts productive.

I would suggest if at all possible, you read these together. One reads while the other listens. It opens up times of discussion and is one way you can spend some of that together-time profitably. But if that is not at all possible, an alternate way is for one spouse to read the first chapter, and the other to then read the same chapter. Alternate each chapter that way. Then when you are together, have a discussion time over what you've read. What helped you, perhaps what you didn't agree with and why, etc. In other words, make this as interactive as you possibly can. Don't one of you read it through, then the other and not really dig into the book or interact with each other over what insights and questions the book revealed.

7) Be willing to give "trust on loan" to the unfaithful spouse. This is a concept I came up with shortly after discovery day. Here's what it is, what it isn't, and why I think it is important.

Trust on loan simply means that I am granting a certain level of trust to the unfaithful spouse. It doesn't mean I trust the unfaithful spouse. It only means if rebuilding is going to succeed, I'll have to trust him to some degree or another. Because no matter how much checking I do, spying, or other activities the hurt spouses tend to do to verify that his unfaithful spouse is staying true, if the unfaithful spouse wants to, he can get back with the affair partner and learn to hide it that much better. If you caught him by using a key logger on his computer, he'll stop using his computer for any type of contact. If you spotted problems in the phone bill, he may get a secret second phone. If you caught him in a certain location, he'll make sure they only are together in a more secluded area. In most cases, the hurt spouse will not be able to eliminate all opportunities and monitor the unfaithful spouse day in and day out enough to ensure he has absolutely no chance to cheat. One spouse reported her husband cheated on her by having lunch-break fun with a co-worker at his job in the parking lot. How would you know about that short of hiring a private detective to follow him around all day?

But what it doesn't mean is you're giving the unfaithful spouse trust like he had prior to the affair. The key is it is "on loan," which means it has to be repaid. He repays it by doing the things that rebuild trust. But he will default on that loan if he violates that trust again. So the trust is not blind trust. It doesn't mean the hurt spouse isn't going to verify. Rather, it is like President Ronald Reagan said, "Trust but verify." If the verification shows a default on that loan, then the borrower is in deep, hot water, and is certainly not shown to be cooperative.

But giving them this loan is also a level of hope for the unfaithful spouse. It means there's an end to this somewhere down the road. A point at which the hurt spouse will feel the loan is paid back. Don't think that will mean you'll feel the same type of trust you had prior to the affair. That trust level is forever lost. You cannot and should never return to that type of trust. Rather, it will be a cautious trust. A trust born out of respect for the temptations and human weaknesses we all bear. When red flags pop up, they will be given stronger attention and concern than they ever did prior to the affair.

For the hurt spouse, it really is what you'll have to do anyway simply by matter of necessity. However, stating it up front with the unfaithful spouse like this will do two things. One, it will make it clear with the unfaithful spouse that while you're giving them room, if they are not diligent, it could end up being room enough to hang themselves. They are rebuilding on borrowed trust. Not free trust. They blew that with the affairs, and now they have to earn it back, loan or no loan.

Two, it will provide some sense of the hurt spouse letting go by handing them some level of trust. You'll check on them, but maybe you won't obsess over it as much. If they are truly being a cooperative unfaithful spouse, they will take this opportunity to pay back that loan because they want that trust back.

When my unfaithful spouse was given this loan, she stated earning it back. One of the primary ways she earned it back was twofold. One, she's been totally transparent. Two, she's told me things she could have easily hidden from me and I'd never known. Mostly about times her affair partner has tried to contact her. Even yesterday in writing this, she reported to me an incident when the affair partner pulled up beside her and waved at her. She could have said nothing to me and I'd never known the difference. If they were getting back together, she would have never told me this information. But she told me as soon as she returned home. By doing this, she pays off the loan each time it happens, because it is evidence she's being honest.

8) Pray together. If you are spiritually oriented, participate together in your religion's spiritual disciplines. For a long time, I would go to Saturday night services by myself. It is a 45 minute trip there and another 45 back. She always felt it more important to not miss TV shows, or just too much to get dinner ready and go to church. But after discovery day, she goes to church with me nearly every time I go. Not just Sunday mornings like it used to be. Not only does she get the spiritual time with me, we can also talk and read our books on the way there and back.

If you've been lax in your faith, but you do have faith, now is a good time to refocus on that together. It can not only help develop closer spiritual bonds with each other, but provide more time together and can be a social outlet with other people as well. Don't forget, a good marriage has a strong bond spiritually as well as emotionally and physically. For the same reasons focusing on strengthening your marriage will help rebuilding to succeed, so will strengthening your spiritual bonds.

Some of the same principles listed above for strengthen the marriage apply toward strengthening the spiritual bonds. Talk to your pastor/priest/spiritual leader as it concerns your faith. If you fear the ostracizing of the unfaithful spouse, go to a neighboring spiritual leader you trust. Get some spiritual counseling in dealing with the affair constructively. Likewise, reading good spiritually enriching books together can be helpful as well.

9) Show thankfulness. A cooperative unfaithful spouse is a blessing for a hurt spouse. Too often the unfaithful spouse wants to hide from his responsibility, or sweep everything under the rug and not talk about it. Or he becomes so busy, he finds it easier to avoid dealing with the issues by not giving them or you time to focus on it. To have an unfaithful spouse who fully cooperates means healing can happen easier and faster for both of you. The more the unfaithful spouse feels you are appreciative of his efforts and struggles, the easier it will be for him to face the more difficult aspects of what he is dealing with.

10) Don't forget to focus on yourself. If the unfaithful spouse is fully cooperative, it means nothing if you get stuck in a bad place. Often hurt spouses get stuck because something has been swept under the rug and not dealt with. Frequently it is the unfaithful spouse that does this, but sometimes the unfaithful spouse can do everything right, but the hurt spouse can't get past a stage of grieving and fails to heal. Go back to the general steps and make sure you are doing them, and working through the stages of grief so that you can arrive at acceptance. Once that takes place, you are in sync with the unfaithful spouse and can take what they are doing in a more constructive manner. But if due to not guarding your thoughts, or remaining angry because you've been wronged, and unable to forgive enough to let go of the righteous indignation, rebuilding will be greatly hindered.

As mentioned previously, if you're going to rebuild, commit yourself to it. You'll have to trust that the unfaithful spouse is working on his end. What you don't want to happen is to get lax in your own efforts so that he heals and you don't. Then the marriage is still in danger and all the work of rebuilding will have been for naught.

Other steps could be added, but these should cover most of the bases on dealing with a cooperative unfaithful spouse so that you give both of you the best chance to succeed in the rebuilding efforts. Next up will be the steps in dealing with an uncooperative unfaithful spouse.

Healing Steps for the Hurt Spouse – Uncooperative Unfaithful Spouse

In the two previous articles, we've discussed the general healing steps for the hurt spouse, and the healing steps for the hurt spouse who has a cooperative unfaithful spouse. Now we want to turn our attention to the healing steps a hurt spouse can do when their unfaithful partner isn't so cooperative.

Keep in mind what we mean by cooperative, and how sometimes there are gray areas. But in general, he is uncooperative if he is not doing most of the healing steps for the unfaithful spouse, like being transparent, maintaining no contact with the affair partner(s), being willing to answer the hurt spouse's questions and concerns, etc. In other words, he is doing more rug sweeping, blame-shifting, and excuse making than working to face and deal with the affair issues head on.

When an unfaithful spouse isn't cooperative, many of the steps outlined in dealing with a cooperative unfaithful spouse will either not be effective or perhaps counterproductive. Consider the following example. You come down with cancer. After some screenings and tests, the doctor says that the cancer is spreading through the breast. So he recommends waiting to see what it will do.

"What?" you may say. "You're crazy! Operate now and cut out that breast before it spreads further!" Wait very long, and the patient isn't likely to survive. But what if the doctor said instead, "There is some cancer, but it appears to be in remission. Still, I recommend cutting out the breast." Well, that isn't much better. If it is in remission, wait and see if it goes away on its own, or gets localized enough that a simple surgery to remove the mass will effectively get rid of it. No need to lose the breast when you don't need to.

In short, the treatment for a more severe situation wouldn't work so well with a "cooperative" cancer, and likewise the treatment for a less serious cancerous situation would be too little, too late for a severe situation. The treatment should match the situation. Same for this.

Using these steps on a cooperative unfaithful spouse could backfire, causing them to lose hope. While using the steps for a cooperative unfaithful spouse on an uncooperative unfaithful spouse will either do little to promote good healing, or could make the unfaithful spouse think everything is going good when it isn't. The hurt spouse could end up sending the wrong signals to the unfaithful spouse.

The goal of these steps is to move an uncooperative unfaithful spouse into being a cooperative unfaithful spouse. In other words, if these steps are successful, they will be temporary and not long term solutions. Once the unfaithful spouse starts being cooperative in an area, you will want to shift to the cooperative steps, at least for that one area.

The only situation where these become permanent is if the unfaithful spouse doesn't respond, never becomes cooperative, and the marriage ends in divorce. That possibility should be kept in mind. There are no guarantees that an uncooperative unfaithful spouse will respond positively to these steps and become cooperative. If he is too far gone, he may push further away instead of change course. In which case, there is little you could have done anyway.

However, there is another goal in these steps. We spoke of it in the general steps. You want to approach the uncooperative unfaithful spouse with the same attitude and control as with a cooperative: using respect, confidence, and a sense of your own security established, even if you don't feel it is there. These steps help you to take a reasoned approach and response. If you react with yelling, fighting, extreme emotions, that will not be effective in demonstrating the attitude needed to convince the unfaithful spouse that he needs to take stock and change course. Let him yell and show anger. But if you remain calm, collected, and controlled, what signal does that send?

One, you are serious and not playing around. He either gets on board or he's going to find himself one spouse short. Nothing is more unsettling than someone stating something serious without yelling. Think of Clint Eastwood's Dirty Harry. He didn't yell it, but you knew he was about to pull trigger if you pressed him when he said, "Go ahead, make my day." It will be even more unsettling if your normal mode of operation has been to yell and fight when these subjects come up. It will say to your spouse, "I'm done playing games. This is it."

Two, it shows that you are not making decisions based on emotion, but reasoned thought. If you are yelling, he'll figure you'll get over it. You're just flying off the handle, and you'll change your mind within an hour or day of cooling off. But if there is no emotional display, he will realize this comes from something deeper than just being hurt, but an inner decision that you are emotionally disconnecting from him. He is no longer worth getting angry about. That will create even more unnerving because it sends a clear signal to the uncooperative unfaithful spouse that the time clock is ticking, and he'll either need to make a strong commitment and stick to it, or watch as the train pulls out of the station without him.

It might help if we look at it using the analogy Shirley Glass uses in *Not Just Friends*. In that book, she uses the analogy of windows to show how even an emotional affair ends up stealing intimacy from one's spouse. For when an unfaithful spouse opens a window to another person that should only be opened to his spouse, he will end up closing that window to his spouse. Each secret is a window closed, and each transparency point a window opened into his soul. When he opens a window to another person that he knows his spouse would not approve of, he'll tend to hide it from her, closing her off to that part of his life. Because of that, the unfaithful spouse distances himself from their spouse, even if he never tells and the spouse never finds out. He ends up having a dark secret that he won't tell the person he's supposed to be closest to.

Take that concept, and put it in the hands of the hurt spouse. By closing some windows on the unfaithful spouse, you are communicating to him two things.

One, that you are reflecting the reality of the situation. He is closed off to you, so you respond by closing off from him. The more open he is with you, the more open you are with him. The more closed off he stays, the more closed off you become. You are simply reflecting reality back to them.

Two, you are creating in him a feeling of distance from you. This realization of a growing distance between you convinces him of something many unfaithful spouses have told themselves wouldn't happen in their affair fog: their spouse will leave them. When they begin to get the sense it is headed down that road, it serves as a wake up call for many unfaithful spouses. What they didn't think would happen is happening, and the abstract idea turns into a concrete reality. Failing to make a commitment to rebuild ends up making the decision to leave if he doesn't act. That is exactly what you want to accomplish. To stop the rug sweeping of the issues and force him to face and deal with them so that healing can move forward. Because until that happens, not much else can.

You'll see some relationship between these steps and the 180: a series of steps to help someone recovering from an affair. The same principles apply there as they do here, to hopefully move the unfaithful spouse to a more cooperative posture with the hurt spouse in healing, and if not, to emotionally prepare the hurt spouse for the eventual separation. So here are the steps I'd recommend a hurt spouse take if you've determined that your unfaithful spouse is not being cooperative in rebuilding:

1) Respond to emotional distance with emotional distance. As mentioned above, it communicates the reality to the unfaithful spouse. It often isn't easy to see what you are doing or communicating to another person until that same message gets communicated back to you. What you don't want to communicate to the unfaithful spouse is that everything is okay. That is unfortunately what many hurt spouses end up communicating. They try to win the unfaithful spouse back, which only pushes them away further. Why? Because that affection either rings as not true ("How could you feel that way after what I did to you?") or as confirming that he is on the right track because he is being rewarded for the path he is on.

The bulk of the 180's suggestions are designed with this idea in mind. Don't call him frequently, don't talk about the future, don't plan dates with him, etc. Instead, you make as little contact as possible and when you do, stick to the business at hand or the kids. Avoid any conversations about the relationship or where it is going. Only open up as much as he opens up to you. If he opens a window, you open a window. If he shuts one, you shut one.

2) Be clear and honest in how you feel. That might seem to be going against the first, but not really. When he does open a window, be clear in your feelings. Avoid blaming, pointing fingers, but say what you really feel. Don't pull any punches. You don't want to beat around the bush about how you feel when the opportunity arises to do so. But again, convey them in as unemotional a manner as you can. Think of Sargent Friday's "Just the facts, ma'am" attitude and demeanor. If the unfaithful spouse starts responding in anger or blame-shifting, all you need to say is, "I don't agree, I'm only telling you how I feel." He can't really argue with how you feel. You feel what you feel. If he doesn't know how you feel, he can't be expected to adapt himself to address it.

3) Schedule some events without the spouse. Schedule an outing with friends or relatives. Don't set up any kind of dating relationship. Avoid feeling like you want to get back at him by showing him how it feels. It is too easy for you to end up falling into she same trap as he did and puts you on his level, greatly complicating any chance of rebuilding and saving the marriage. But do go out and have some fun without him by your side. It will send him the clear message that you will be able to have fun and move on with your life without the unfaithful spouse if that's what it comes to.

4) Separate your financial accounts. Set up and fund your own bank account that your spouse doesn't have access to. Add money to it regularly as a financial security blanket. This has a practical as well as motivational basis. Not only does it make clear that you are becoming more independent, but if the unfaithful spouse doesn't become cooperative and the marriage comes to an end, you won't be left holding an empty money bag.

Additionally, in many cases the unfaithful spouse is spending money on the affair partner. Sequestering some or most of the money away ensures he won't end up spending it all and leaving you with unpaid bills. "But won't he be doing the same thing?" Yes, and it is likely he has already done so before you found out about the affair, in order to hide his spending and tipping you off about the hotel bills you don't know about. Because he is doing that, you need your own as well. Remember, respond in equal portion to the degree he is responding to you.

5) Have an initial consultation with a lawyer. "But I don't believe in divorce," you may respond. "I don't need to do that step." You may not believe in it, but that doesn't mean your spouse won't push you into one. It takes two to make a marriage, and if one spouse has given up, for whatever reason, no amount of not believing is going to stop the divorce from happening.

What you want to do here is prepare for the worst. The unfaithful spouse doesn't even need to know you've done this. But if push comes to shove and the divorce comes, either because you or the unfaithful spouse decide he wants out and won't consider anything else, you need to be aware of your options legally in your state and/or country. If you don't know, you are at a disadvantage if and when it happens. As long as the unfaithful spouse is uncooperative, the possibility of ending in divorce is always present. Better to be prepared and not need to use that information than to be caught flatfooted and lose some important concessions you could have had.

6) Assume the unfaithful spouse is still cheating. The only way you can be assured that the unfaithful spouse is maintaining no contact and the affair is over is if he is totally transparent and ready to talk about it. If he is hiding anything, it is a sure sign he doesn't want you to see something incriminating. He'll say it will hurt you, which is all the more reason to consider the affair still ongoing. Until the unfaithful spouse becomes cooperative, there is no way to verify that the affair is over. There is no trust level that the hurt spouse can have in any statements by the unfaithful spouse to the contrary.

If the affair is really over, his actions would demonstrate that. You can't believe any denial of a continuing affair until he's proved himself by opening up his full life to you without reservation. Even then, it will take some time for the hurt spouse to stop feeling like he might still be cheating. But as long as he is closed off and uncooperative, assume he is still cheating. Then future revelations will not be such a surprise and you will keep a real distance from him that reflects the reality.

7) Refrain from a sexual relationship with the unfaithful spouse and get tested for STDs. This one goes along with #1 above, in that obviously if you are creating emotional distance, refraining from sex is one way to do that. But it can be one of the harder to do depending on the person and has more consequences, which is why I'm highlighting it.

First, if the possibility exists that he is still cheating (see #6), then you do not want to reward the unfaithful spouse by also having sex with them. He needs to know that he cannot have both. Until you feel secure that the affair has ended, it would be counter-productive for you to continue a normal sexual relationship with him. Because sex is a commitment to another person, whether he means it that way or not, to be bonded with him, to have children with him. Because even in the most careful situations there is always the possibility of a child that binds the two together. Even an abortion doesn't erase that fact. Having sex with someone other than one's spouse destroys that bond with the spouse. Until you can know you are the only one, it is destructive to the other spouse to continue to give yourself to him sexually.

But the more practical reason is also because if the unfaithful spouse is still sleeping with others, there is the potential at any time, if not already true, that he could pass an STD to you from someone else. Even with a cooperative unfaithful spouse it is a good idea to get tested for any STDs, but especially if you feel he hasn't ended the affair yet. If you do have any STDs from the affair(s), it could be a bone of contention in any possible divorce proceedings. If the tests don't reveal any STDs, you at least don't want to continue subjecting yourself to the "Russian Roulette" of the STD gun by continuing to have sex with your spouse. Not until you are confident he has stopped any relationship with another, has been tested for STDs, and is clean.

When you do feel the unfaithful spouse is ready to commit to a totally exclusive relationship with you again, make it clear that by having sex with you, that he is making an irrevocable commitment to you of fidelity, and that failure to keep that will have serious consequences as far as the marriage goes.

"But what if you believe they've had only had an emotional affair and there was no sexual relationship?" First, can you really trust that he hasn't? Many unfaithful spouses do the "trickle truth" where they don't tell you everything up front, so they'll say they talked, maybe held hands, but didn't have sex. But then in a few months you find out evidence they met in a hotel room, or other piece of evidence that suggests the likelihood of a sexual relationship was high.

Keep in mind, we're only talking here about an uncooperative unfaithful spouse, not a cooperative one. If he is still hiding things from you, the likelihood he has told you everything is slim. If he is not being cooperative, you can only assume he is still hiding the full story from you, and you'll have to assume there was physical contact until the time you feel fairly confident there wasn't. Which usually doesn't happen until some months have passed in a healthy rebuilding with a cooperative unfaithful spouse. Once the unfaithful spouse has become cooperative and has made a firm commitment to rebuilding the marriage and not being with anyone else, only then can the hurt spouse feel confident in resuming sexual relations with him.

Second, an emotional affair in most cases involves mental adultery. That is, even when one has refrained from sex with an affair partner, there is usually an inner desire to do so, whether it ever gets fulfilled or not. Sometimes it is denied by the unfaithful spouse even to themselves, but other times it is a conscious thought, "I would love to get her in bed."

My wife sex chatted with several men during her affairs. I happened to read through some of the communications she had on MySpace. One in particular she sounded like she was ready to hop into bed with him. When I told her about that, she denied it. Said she would have never done anything with him, and didn't think she encouraged him. I told her she most certainly did encourage him. When she went back and read the message in question, she couldn't believe it. She literally had told him when he talked about coming to our city to meet her and what he would do to her sexually, that she would really like that experience. She hadn't realized at the time just how much she really sounded like she wanted to have him.

But the fact is, if there is desire, it is an adulterous affair even if the deed is never done. Even if the person only liked their company, spending that amount of time texting and talking, having much more intimate communication than with his spouse opens a marital window to someone other than his spouse and is moving toward the eventual destination of at least wanting to have sex with this person, if not actually doing it.

8) Use separation if needed. Sometimes it is hard to establish minimal contact with the unfaithful spouse due to tight living quarters, both working from home, or other issues. It is generally recommended if you find yourself in shouting fights with the unfaithful spouse and hard to avoid them, a time of separation is in order.

The downsides to separation are you can no longer keep track of the unfaithful spouse's activities as before. There is no easy way short of hiring a private investigator to keep watch over his apartment, to know that his affair partner isn't stopping by for regular visits. He is free to go out on the town and stay out until the wee hours of the morning without worrying that you'll find out about it.

Even if the affair partner is sleeping over, there is one reality that the unfaithful spouse experiences in all of this: what life will be like without the spouse and the children, if any. It may take a while, but at some point he'll feel the loss of his marriage and the kids. That can also get contrasted with the now easily available affair partner. Waking up to them may not be as exciting as those secret meetings in the night.

I wouldn't try this first thing, but if putting some emotional distance between you yields no significant results, then if it simply hasn't sunk into the unfaithful spouse's head that the marriage train is about to leave the station and he hasn't boarded it, this can make that reality more real. A final warning shot over his bow saying, "I'm not waiting much longer. Either get aboard or it's bye bye." If a separation doesn't wake him up, then there's not much that will.

If he decides to come back from a separation, this is your opportunity to lay out the conditions for their return. Write down a "contract" of sorts, listing out your expectations, the length of time any will last if applicable, and what happens if the unfaithful spouse fails to live up to those expectations. It is easy to say, "Yes, I'll be transparent," but much harder when the hurt spouse has their hand out, wanting their cell phone, to give it to him because the unfaithful spouse may have some embarrassing material on it. Once he is back in the house, it will be much easier for him to go back on their commitment thinking you won't really follow through or throw them out for it. So be prepared to do just that, should it come down to it.

What you don't want to do is have him come back in without extracting some serious commitments about how things are going to be. The only way to move them to being a cooperative unfaithful spouse is to establish the steps he'll need to take to get there. Moving back in from a separation is the most leverage you will have as a hurt spouse to accomplish that goal. Don't waste it.

9) Reward movement toward being cooperative. Assuming these steps have the desired affect, and the unfaithful spouse becomes cooperative, respond by also opening that window so that he will know he is on the right track. But you may need to open the window slowly, in shifts, until it is fully open.

For example, let's say the unfaithful spouse has been reluctant to become fully transparent. But due to you not being full transparent with the unfaithful spouse, he begins to realize if he wants to keep you, he needs to do that. So he lets you see his cell phone, text messages, Facebook account, giving you the passwords, etc. Let's say you set up that private bank account. You may at that point decide to tell him that you have it. You might avoid telling him at what bank, or how much is in it, or any other details. But you've cracked the window open.

Then a couple of weeks down the road, you discover a secret Facebook account that he didn't tell you about. You shut the window back down and say nothing more about the bank account. Wouldn't even hurt to use a little gas lighting on them, "I never said anything about a bank account. You must have been dreaming." Or maybe after a couple of weeks, it appears nothing new has come about, and you can find no evidence of further hiding, you might reveal which bank the account is at. And so on.

You may not want to use a secret bank account to start with, this was just an example of what I meant by opening the window in phases and rewarding the unfaithful spouse. It could be anything, to more willingness to discuss the marriage, to sharing your email and Facebook passwords as well. As he moves in the right directions, you want to reward him by opening your own windows in response to him opening his. Remember that a window open to you is one closed to the affair partner.

10) Keep the goals in sight, and avoid shifting to new one's. What I mean by this is sometimes in dealing with these type of steps to gain emotional distance in response to the unfaithful spouse's emotional distance, it can lead a hurt spouse to shift their goal from saving the marriage to getting out of it. Sometimes it is a subtle shift, but a shift nonetheless.

You can detect it when you fail to respond to the unfaithful spouse's positive advances in being cooperative. Instead of opening windows, you keep them shut. The emotional distance can feel like freedom to a hurt spouse filled with anger, who is having trouble dealing with the reality of what the unfaithful spouse did. The hurt spouse may find safety in not depending on the spouse for their sense of security. In the beginning days, it is natural to feel that way. He's hurt you, and you don't trust him to not do it again. So when he makes that movement to more honesty and openness, it isn't easy for the hurt spouse to feel good about opening himself up in response.

But when the hurt spouse stays there for weeks, months, or even years, whether he has consciously made a decision to rebuild or not, it is in effect a decision to end the marriage. Just as an unfaithful spouse needs to be cooperative for rebuilding and healing to work, so does a hurt spouse need to cooperate and respond with the unfaithful spouse. If the goal to help the unfaithful spouse move toward being cooperative and rebuilding the marriage is lost sight of, and the hurt spouse gets stuck in the security of being distant so he doesn't get hurt again, that is in effect a decision to end the marriage. It might take a while, but at some point the unfaithful spouse will give up and the marriage will end.

Unfaithful spouses need to be aware that it may take the hurt spouse some time to deal with what has happened to him. These are situations that take months to heal, and that's if everything is done to heal as discussed earlier. If it takes a few months for the unfaithful spouse to open up and be transparent, willing to discuss all aspects of the affair until the hurt spouse is satisfied, and for the unfaithful spouse to really accept his responsibility in the affair and work diligently to heal himself, that adds onto the time it will take for the hurt spouse to heal. For he can't heal until the affair is over. For the hurt spouse, it isn't over until he feels it is over.

That said, hurt spouses have a responsibility if they have committed to rebuilding the marriage. It isn't a good idea to say, "Yes, I'm willing to rebuild," but then when it comes down to it, shift goals on the unfaithful spouse. There are always things that the hurt spouse doesn't anticipate, feelings he didn't realize he would have. Obsessive thoughts that he has a hard time dealing with. Those are all going to happen, and if the unfaithful spouse is fully on board with rebuilding, he will expect and stay with you as you go through them. But if the hurt spouse stands in the way of healing, at some point the unfaithful spouse will lose hope and stop trying.

If, however, you keep the goals in mind when you are doing these steps, they will become ways to help the unfaithful spouse see your seriousness about the broken marriage and get serious himself, and if possible, move him from an uncooperative unfaithful spouse to a cooperative one. Because the ultimate goal is healing, and an uncooperative unfaithful spouse will not bring healing.

That concludes the three articles on the "Healing Steps for the Hurt Spouse. They are not intended to be comprehensive by any means, but will give the hurt spouse some stepping stones to further progress and perspectives to see the next steps to be taken.

Also, use these steps in the three articles at your own risk. That is, these are my best steps to healing, but there are no guarantees when dealing with people, nor can I foresee every possible outcome from using these steps. They may or may not work for any one individual situation. Each person, knowing their circumstances and those involved, should evaluate and use them at their discretion, and preferably with the aid of a counselor. But I think in general, these are the paths to healing for the hurt spouse. I pray they will be helpful.

Healing Through Forgiveness

Forgiveness is one of the often difficult steps that a person hurt by the infidelity of a spouse can take. In part because the betrayal of the unfaithful partner is a deep hurt. The trust is placed in one's spouse, the commitment made to each other and to God, leaves us open to that deep hurt. The more on guard we are, the less likely someone's betrayal of our trust will hurt us. The less intimate the relationship between two people, the more walls and defenses we put up to guard against such attacks.

But we don't expect such attacks from those who love us. The risk one takes when one love another and are intimate with him is that any hurts go deep. They strike us at our very core and affect our self-esteem and identity. So it is no wonder that when such a deep hurt has been inflicted upon someone, that they find it difficult to forgive. Yet, for full healing to take place, that is exactly what needs to happen. So let's look at the process of forgiveness in relation to the hurt inflicted by the infidelity of one's spouse.

First, let's define what forgiveness is. Webster defines it: "To pardon; to remit, as an offense or debt; to overlook an offense, and treat the offender as not guilty." The two ingredients, in this context, are an offense committed against you and the release from punishment for it.

There are some who speak of "earning forgiveness." This is a contradictory statement. One cannot earn forgiveness, for by its very definition it is an act of mercy. For example, if I owe a debt to a creditor, and they decide to forgive me that debt, that means I don't need to pay it back. If I earn that money back and pay the debt off, then there is no need to forgive me the debt. One can't earn forgiveness. As soon as you do, it is no longer forgiveness by definition.

What I believe people really mean by that statement isn't conditions upon which a spouse will forgive the unfaithful spouse, but the conditions upon which the unfaithful spouse can receive that forgiveness and benefit from it for saving the marriage. We'll examine that in a minute, but in this case the unfaithful spouse doesn't "earn" it, it is what he needs to do to apply the forgiveness to themselves.

For example, let's say you need to hammer in a nail, but you don't have a hammer or anything that will work for one. But your good friend holds out a hammer for you to use. In reaching out your hand and taking that hammer, have you "earned" that use of the hammer? Of course not. Neither is doing the actions to receive forgiveness earning it. It is simply holding out your hand.

Likewise, that the spouse has to do those things to receive forgiveness doesn't have any bearing on whether the hurt spouse forgives or not. We examine why below, but just as God stands always ready to forgive, so are we called to do, no matter what the offender does or doesn't do.

There are some natural conclusions that can be drawn from this understanding that we'll address as we go through this information. But first, it may be helpful to address what forgiveness is not.

One, forgiveness is not a denial of the wrongness or hurt that an action brought about. Notice the above definition. It says, "treat the offender as not guilty." It doesn't say the offender isn't guilty, but you are going to treat him as not guilty by way of not punishing him. In truth, it acknowledges that you do have a right to punish him because of his offense. If you didn't, there would be no point to forgiveness. Forgiveness is an act of mercy on your part, not a denial of the offense itself.

Two, forgiveness does not mean the offender will not be punished. What it means is you are not going to do the punishing! A sin like adultery hurts the adulterer as much, if not more, than the hurt spouse. That may seem contradictory as we tend to think, "He had the fun at my expense!" But adultery isn't a sin because it is fun to do. It is a sin because it causes some very serious damage to one's soul and life. That is why Paul said in 1 Corinthians 6:18, "Flee fornication. Every sin that a man does is outside the body, but he who commits fornication sins against his own body."

Three, forgiveness does not erase the consequences of the offense. As mentioned above, by showing mercy and forgiving the offender, it only means you will not add your punishment to the natural consequences he will endure. Take the example of King David. He committed adultery and murder to cover up his sin. Psalm 51 is an example of what true repentance is about. According to the Scriptures, God forgave David. But he still had consequences due to that sin. The baby that resulted from that sin died. His sons ended up fighting and dividing the kingdom, even rebelling against David.

David suffered the consequences of his sin. So will the unfaithful partner suffer for their sins, even though God and you forgive them.

But by this point, one might ask, why is it necessary to forgive to heal? Isn't part of healing that justice is served? Shouldn't he know I'm not going to put up with this behavior? Won't forgiving the offender be sending the message, "I'm not offended or hurt"?

There is a difference between not putting up with a behavior, and the message of forgiveness. As noted above, forgiveness does not negate the consequences of his actions. One of those consequences, if he persists in his sin, is the loss of his spouse. Forgiveness is not a "Get out of jail free" card, rather it is both an opportunity for the offender to change his behavior before worse consequences set in, and the release of the offended from their own sins.

If the offended spouse were to mitigate the consequences of the sin, and not merely forgive, then that would be sending the wrong signal. It is one thing to say, "I'm not going to beat you over the head with this offense you've committed against me for the rest of our lives," but quite another to say, "I will stay by your side and support you, no matter how often you have an affair." One can forgive the spouse for his infidelity even while separating from him because the spouse refuses to give up his infidelity. This allows you to forgive, but not enable his sin by erasing the negative consequences of it.

But forgiveness is more about you than about the offender. It is his opportunity to repent and make right the wrongs he's committed against you. But you can no more control his responses to your forgiveness than you could prevent him from cheating on you. All you really have under your control is yourself. Forgiveness is absolutely necessary for the healing of the offended much more than it is about healing for the offender.

For one who will not forgive is also one who is not forgiven for his own sins. Jesus states this clearly in the parable of the servant who owed his master so much money, there was no way he could ever pay it off even if he worked for the rest of his life. The master forgave the servant the debt. But the servant, either not accepting that he'd been forgiven or too selfish himself, refused to forgive someone who owed him a small amount of money, and had him thrown into prison. The master, upon hearing this, reinstated the money the ungrateful servant had been forgiven because he refused to forgive. Jesus' conclusion to the parable was, "Thus also My heavenly Father will do to you, if you do not forgive each one his brother their trespasses, from your hearts." (Mat 18:35 EMTV).

Jesus also states this clearly in the Lord's Prayer, when we ask

God to "forgive us our trespasses as we forgive those who trespass against us." By refusing to forgive, we cut off the grace for our own forgiveness from God. This is because forgiveness is like a river of running water. For the river to flow for you, it must flow for those down the line. That is in part why in the early Church, the prescription for baptizing someone was, if at all possible, to do so in running water. Sins are washed away by the flow of grace. Stop the flow, and you have stagnant water that grows stale and dirty.

It should be noted that this is not so much God saying, "What? You won't forgive? Well, then, I'll show you!" No, God is always ready to forgive. But what happens is if you cannot forgive others, it demonstrates you are unable to receive the forgiveness that God offers. It is like you have the faucet open and water is coming out, and you are drinking it, but the moment someone else wants that water from you, you shut it off so they cannot get any. But then, neither can you get any. So in your refusal to give someone your forgiveness, you cut it off for yourself as well.

It is for this reason that when the woman caught in adultery was put before Jesus by the Pharisees, attempting to trap Jesus, He replied that he who is without sin should cast the first stone. Because they had sins that needed forgiveness, they either forgave her or stood condemned themselves. They all forgave her, and so did Jesus. (John 8:3-11)

Therefore, forgiving is necessary for your own healing, but it is also necessary for the healing of the marriage, if there is to be a chance for that to happen. Forgiveness takes the bitterness and hate off your shoulders for what the other person did to you. If you are going to rebuild the marriage, one key component of that rebuilding is to release yourself from the anger and hate for what they did to you. As long as that is festering, it will not be possible to restore the relationship.

This is why God Himself forgives us in order to restore our relationship with Him. If God was not willing to forgive, there would be no hope for us but death. But because He is willing, there is hope for eternal life with Him. So it is for the spouse. If a spouse remains bitter and hateful to the other, rebuilding will be impossible and the marriage will suffer. Healing will not take place.

For these reasons, it is necessary for the hurt spouse to heal within themselves, and for the marriage to be healed, as well as releasing the unfaithful spouse to have opportunity to heal, that we must seek to forgive the individuals in the affair.

Even the affair partner. You need to forgive them for your own healing. For the bitterness and hate it can generate will poison your spirit and will carry over to the unfaithful spouse. The affair partner is an easy target since you are not reconciling with him, and you hope to never see or speak to him. But the unfaithful spouse and the affair partner, in most all cases, willingly participated together, even if one seduced the other or took advantage of the other's weakness. Hate for the affair partner will transfer to the unfaithful spouse by the fact that he or she joined with him against you. So even harboring unforgiveness toward the affair partner while forgiving the unfaithful spouse will block rebuilding efforts.

This is often seen when the inability to forgive results in the hurt spouse's obsessions over the affair partner, seeking revenge on him, or wanting to punish him. It puts the focus on the affair partner and the wrongs he committed against you and the marriage, instead of on the marriage and working with your unfaithful spouse to heal it. The best way to focus on the marriage and its healing is to forgive the affair partner and then take them off the radar screen.

What about forgiving yourself? Sometimes you see an unfaithful spouse talk about their difficulty in forgiving themselves for what they did. But you can't really forgive yourself. You didn't commit the offense against yourself, but against the hurt spouse and God, as well as the affair partner. What most people who ask this are really concerned about is being able to receive forgiveness. They face their guilt, and have trouble believing that anyone really forgives them for that act. They don't accept that their spouse has forgiven them, or that God forgives them. That can result in shame which causes a "death spiral" affect of encouraging the unfaithful spouse to repeat the unfaithfulness. The only way out of that cycle is to come to a place of accepting forgiveness.

There are two aspects of forgiveness as it relates to infidelity that need to be kept in mind. One, that forgiveness is a process and not a one-time event. First, most people will not be ready to forgive upon discovering the affair. Most must go through the stages of grief as it pertains to their loss, and the stages of denial and anger don't lend themselves to an attitude of being ready to forgive. The pain is too fresh and the hurt still being processed to expect an immediate forgiveness. Some can do that, but it is also true that some may short-circuit the grieving process by forgiving too quickly, and in effect end up failing to deal with their anger and hurt. There can be an initial desire to forgive, while not yet knowing all that it entails.

That leads to the other part of the process. We can often think we've forgiven, but then a new layer is peeled back and we must continue to apply forgiveness. We may be faced with the details of what we had forgiven, whereas previously it was generic actions, and feel the hurt once again. Fresh hurt should remind us of our commitment to forgive, and applying that fresh each time to release the bitterness and hate it would engender, and the depression that can trip up rebuilding a marriage.

Two, that forgiveness is only effective in healing the marriage if the unfaithful spouse accepts and allows it to change him and the situation. For the problem has never been whether God will or can forgive us for our sins. No, it has always been about whether we are able to accept His forgiveness. For as long as we are not, His forgiveness does us no good.

That is why God gives the following conditions for His forgiveness to be active in healing us in 2 Chronicles 7:14, and therefore what the unfaithful spouse needs to do for the hurt spouse's forgiveness to be effective in healing the marriage:

Humility – if we do not lower ourselves before God, if we think we know better than He does how to live our life, our pride will prevent us from receiving His forgiveness. Indeed, the one key to why most people cannot receive forgiveness nor give forgiveness is their own pride. Pride says, "I don't need your forgiveness, I'm right," to God, and to those we've offended, "My rights have been violated, and I will be given what is due me in retribution." If the unfaithful spouse maintains an attitude of pride and not owning their responsibility in the affair, no forgiveness will be received by the unfaithful spouse.

Pray – if we do not ask, due to that pride, if we do not make request for forgiveness, it shows our unbelief that the offended is or can forgive us. It means you don't believe the forgiver when he says, "I forgive you for what you did to me." So you refuse to even ask for it.

Seek my face – if we do not face the one we've offended and look them in the eye, if we refuse to face the guilt in our lives and desire mercy for what we've done, if we avoid him, don't want to talk about it, ignore him, then we cannot receive his forgiveness and have it be active in healing us and the marriage.

Turn from your wicked ways – if the unfaithful spouse refuses to stop the affair by making no further contact with the affair partner(s), is more concerned about the feelings of the affair partner than he is about his own spouse, if he continues the affair or returns to it, and does not stop doing that which is hurting his spouse and destroying their marriage, the hurt spouse can forgive all he wants, but it will do no good for healing of the marriage. To not stop is to say, in pride, "I am not wrong. I want to do this, my way."

If these things are done, however, we are promised that God will forgive our sins and heal our land. If the hurt spouse is able to get to the point of offering forgiveness to the unfaithful spouse, unless the unfaithful spouse is doing the above, he will not be helped by his spouse's forgiveness nor will he and the marriage be healed.

Forgiveness is not an option if the goal is healing of the hurt spouse, the unfaithful spouse, and the marriage itself. While the hurt spouse may not be ready to forgive immediately, it does have to happen at some point in the healing process for the relationship to be restored as it should be. Additionally, the unfaithful partner needs to do the things necessary to receive that forgiveness or they put their own healing and that of the marriage in jeopardy.

Jesus stated it clearly: Then Peter came to Him and said, "Lord, how often shall my brother sin against me, and I forgive him? Up to seven times?" Jesus said to him, "I do not say to you, up to seven times, but up to seventy-seven times." (Mat 18:21-22 EMTV)

To heal, we must forgive and accept forgiveness. It is not an option if the goal is to heal.

Part 4 – General Articles

The Stages of Grief and Infidelity

Both the hurt spouse and the unfaithful spouse go through the stages of grief. Sometimes one or both will get stuck in these stages for various reasons. I am taking the classical stages of grief and applying them to the loss of infidelity to help both hurt spouses and unfaithful spouses understand what they are going through, so you aren't blindsided when these emotions and feeling arise. They are part of the healing process.

These are usually associated with tragedies of various kinds like a death in the family, someone getting cancer, loss of functionality due to an auto accident, etc. The loss of an affair is a little different in that the beginning of grieving toward healing may not be able to get fully underway until the parties involved feel fairly confident that the affair is over, which for some couples can be months, years for the determined, or never.

Hurt spouses suffer the loss of trust, the loss of security in the relationship, the loss of innocence, the loss of who they viewed their spouse to be, loss of feelings of love, if not loving commitment, and other related losses. Many suffer loss of self-esteem because they feel the affair was some deficiency in them, and the spouse must not love them as much as they thought because they chose someone else over them. Additionally, if it ends in divorce, the loss of the whole relationship itself.

The unfaithful spouses will, upon hitting discovery day, at least experience the loss of their secret life, and if they successfully cut off contact, the loss of those relationships. Additionally, they'll experience the loss of their marital intimacy and the trust of their spouse. They'll also experience the loss of their self-respect and self-esteem for what they did (many respond to this in various ways, including denial, shifting guilt, acting like everything is okay, or not wanting to talk about it because they don't enjoy being whipped up on). If it ends in divorce, they also can experience the loss of that relationship.

There are five general stages of grieving most people who suffer loss go through. Not everyone will experience all of these, and they can overlap, or one may feel they've gone beyond one stage only to find themselves back there again. There isn't any neat lines and boxes when one goes from one to the other. You can experience two or three of these things all in one day. But there is a basic progression, and how well you heal from it for yourself (not taking into account any exterior circumstances that could delay or prevent it, like the unfaithful spouse having another affair or the hurt spouse leaving, never to return, etc.) will vary on successfully progressing through these stages.

Denial

This is the usual first stage. The event doesn't seem real. It can't be happening. There must be some explanation. She would never do this to me. Hurt spouses are especially vulnerable to "gas lighting" during this phase, because they are already predisposed to doubt what they are realizing has happened, even with solid proof sitting in front of them. At this stage, the hurt spouse wants to believe there is a reasonable explanation.

I remember my first reaction upon reading Lenita's online confession. I said, "No! No! No!" I had to look away from the computer and sit in a chair, trying to take in what I had just read. It was just so out of character for her, I couldn't believe it was true. Yet, there it was, staring at me in black and white. Though I knew inside it wasn't likely to be the case, I hoped like wildfire that when I confronted her, she would go, "OH! You must have read what I wrote last night to that guy! I was just saying that to play along with him. It was all a big joke." Or, "I knew you installed that key logger and wanted to get back at you. Ha ha! Got you good!" Which would have been a very mean trick, but I would rather that had been the case.

For the unfaithful spouse, the denial may be more along the lines of not believing they'd been caught, and the gig was up. They had convinced themselves that they would never be caught, that they could keep this hidden. Suddenly, that's all falling apart, and for the first time perhaps, they are thinking about what discovery means and its ramifications. But they don't want to consider that. It is what they've hid from for the length of the affair, thinking the two lives could remain separate and not affecting the other. Initially, they may not have wanted the affair to end, and deny that it has, even if he also, at the same time, wants to rebuild with his spouse, which is where much of the ambivalence comes from. They don't want to let go of either life, lose either life, and they are in denial that it has come down to that choice.

Anger

Once it sets in that the affair has happened, and denial is more an emotional disconnect than a mental reality, the anger sets in. For the hurt spouse, the anger is obvious: How could you do this to me? I thought you loved me? You broke our vows! You deceived me! How dare you put my life at risk with unprotected sex behind my back!

The unfaithful spouse can experience anger, even if it appears irrational from the hurt spouse viewpoint: Don't talk about him that way! He is a human too. Why do you keep whipping me about this over and over, I said I was sorry! Why don't you work on yourself more, the marriage isn't all about me? I had needs too! He met them! Pride can easily keep an unfaithful spouse defensive rather than cooperative. He can also be angry at himself or the affair partner for allowing the discovery of the affair.

The point is, both experience loses, and anger is one reaction for many in dealing with the causes or perceived causes of those losses. How easy it is to get over that anger can be due to several factors, including the repentant attitude of the unfaithful spouse, the personality of the hurt spouse, and whether one or both can empathize with the other's feelings of loss. The ability to do the later is usually the opposite of being angry, so the more one is able to look past their own pain and be concerned for the other, the less anger will have a hold.

At some point, the anger begins to feel pointless, as it becomes evident that it is doing more harm to the one who is angry than it is to the other. But in the beginning, the hurt spouse especially feels almost an obligation to be angry, to not appear to let the spouse off "easy." But if it is held onto, it can prevent the hurt spouse from moving toward healing even if the unfaithful spouse does all the proper steps and heals.

Bargaining

One stage some go through is bargaining. This is traditionally thought of in a death loss, usually the person saying something like, "God, if you'll just bring her back, I'll go to the mission field," or some other deal.

In an affair, this is more likely to be reflected in an attempt to get back to the pre-affair life. In hurt spouses, it may be along the lines of "If you'll do these things, I'll stay and rebuild the marriage." Or in drastic cases, the hurt spouse might even say in not so many words, "Just don't flash it before my face, and I'll look the other way. Do what you want as long as you don't leave." Sort of a mixture of denial and bargaining. Or, "God, why did you let this happen to me? Fix him and I'll be the best wife ever."

An "in the fog" unfaithful spouse may think, "If I tell him this much of the truth, I can keep the affair going," or "If I don't tell him everything, I won't have to deal with his hurt and pain, and my shame and guilt." Post-fog unfaithful spouses may say in effect, "If I do everything she wants me to do, be the best husband I can be for a week, six weeks, six months, <insert whatever perceived time frame>, then she'll stay and things will go back to 'normal'." Of course not realizing that this is called "rebuilding," not "remodeling" for a very good reason. What is built back won't look like the original, and it will take a good two years minimum to accomplish under the best of conditions.

Depression

Once the hysterical bonding dies down, and the reality of what is appearing to be the new normal has set in, depression can start to build. Fostered by changing identities, unresolved issues from the affair, or marital issues magnified by the affair, the hurt spouse or unfaithful spouse begins to feel that these are never going to get resolved or fixed. This grows even worse if the hurt spouse discovers continued contact with the affair partner, a new affair has started, or the unfaithful spouse hasn't told him everything and more truth trickles out. The things he thought would "fix" the marriage don't seem to be working, and during this time it can seem the hurt spouse and/or the unfaithful spouse take ten steps back for every step forward.

But even in good rebuilding, when things seem to be going well, there can be a time of depression. It can be experienced early in the process when you are unsure if he is going to break contact with the affair partner, or he doesn't seem repentant, commit to rebuilding like he said, or other related issues. Likewise, later in the process, as you gain perspective with the movement of time, you will look back and lament the losses you've sustained, and that will end up being expressed as depression.

It is in this stage that many couples in rebuilding can hit a wall. The one in depression will appear to have suddenly gone from being hopeful and happy about the marriage to despairing that it will ever work. They lose hope either from being tired of the constant effort and struggle of the rebuilding process with no seeming signs of things getting better, or have unrealistic expectations of how long the rebuilding process would be and how hard it is to go through.

Some will end up giving up at this point, fearing things will never improve or work, and getting out of the marriage is the only solution left. Others can get stuck here for months, even years, effectively halting a full healing and restoration of the relationship. If the couple realizes this for what it is, a natural part of the grieving process, and are patient with each other through it, and work to get past it, it usually leads to the final stage where a fuller healing can begin in earnest.

Acceptance

Here, both parties have come to terms with their losses, and accepted them. They no longer are obsessed with them and desire to look ahead rather than focus on the mess behind them. They are tired of being angry and depressed over it. A new "normal" is on the way to being established and identities formed that offer security and trust strengthened to functioning levels. They have let go of the hurts, that even though they are still there, aren't allowed to guide their lives and rule their thoughts. Forgiveness plays a part in reaching this stage, as injustice and anger is released and replaced with a more optimistic outlook for the future.

The key point becomes, that though it will always be there, the hurt and events of the affair are now considered "in the past" and the focus is on the future, whether one is rebuilding or in a divorced situation. That usually allows the couple to more fully focus on themselves, or the individual on a new relationship to spend their future with.

Hopefully this will be helpful in understanding some of the issues being dealt with by both sides of the affair, and strengthen the chance for healing and rebuilding to be successful.

Am I in Love?

A common statement among unfaithful spouses is that they fell in love with their affair partners. I've heard them say statements like, "She made me feel more alive than I ever have." The rush of an affair-generated love can be addictive. But is the unfaithful spouse really in love with his affair partner? Also what does he mean when he says he still love his spouse despite that?

Likewise, when a hurt spouse discovers the affair, his love for his spouse can take a hit. Some, over time, end up "falling out of love" with their spouse. This causes them to be less motivated in rebuilding or even caring about their spouse. If they stay in the marriage, it is more for the sake of the kids or financial reasons than loving their spouse. Some hurt spouses are unable to ever get over the rejection that the affair caused them to experience, either due to the unfaithful spouse not doing the needed actions to help them heal, or sometimes because the hurt spouse is too wounded from it to heal.

In either case, love or the loss of it becomes involved. It is therefore important that we look at what love is and within the context of an affair and rebuilding, how it can help or hurt as the case may be.

I intend to show why we feel love of various kinds and how they interact to form a full experience of love, and how when extracted from that context, get perverted into a false love. To do this, we need to first understand the four types of loves. C. S. Lewis, in his book "The Four Loves," lists four Greek words most common to understanding love: *storge, philio, eros, and agape.*

I know, I know. Many of you have heard all this before. Before you jump to conclusions about what I'm going to say, press reset for a moment and let's take a fresh look at these in the context of infidelity.

Eros

We're starting with this word because out of the four, it is the most misunderstood word. Perhaps because it is never used in the New Testament, the word tends to be restricted to sexual love. But this is too restrictive, not only in classical Greek usage—Plato uses it in non-sexual contexts—but in the Early Church Fathers, who often used the Greek word, *eros*, to describe our love for God.

The word that sums up the meaning of *eros* is **passion**. It is emotional, and a strong desire that moves us to action. It excites, activates, and moves us to act.

This is the type of love that appeals to help the starving children. Most any appeal, to be successful, has to pull this type of love from you. Seeing pictures of starving children is designed to get you to donate because your pity motivates you, gives you enough passion to move you to act. This is why the Church Fathers used the word in relation to God. We were to have a driving passion for God, and without that, you wouldn't have the motivation to stand up and be martyred for Christ.

Passion itself is a misunderstood term. It comes from the Greek as well and means "to suffer." So the "passion of Christ" refers to the suffering of Christ. How does this get from there to excitement that motivates? Simple. All passion is driven by suffering a lack of something perceived to be needed. In short, when you see something you want, you are suffering because you don't have it. You are in "pain" and are motivated to resolve it by fulfilling that desire.

Added to that, God has built into us a survival mechanism, usually related to hunger and other desires that we need to live. Sex falls into this realm too. When the brain perceives a feeling as pleasurable due to the infusion of dopamine firing off the brain synapses, it stores that as a need. If the dopamine levels are high enough, the brain can rate it as highly needed for survival. This forms the addictive pattern which can eventually—if reinforced enough times—lead one to having an addiction to a specific desire.

This dopamine response pattern can be fooled into perceiving something as a survival need that really is not. Nowhere is this more evident when an unfaithful spouse perceives he can't live without his affair partner, that dumping her means he is missing out on an important part of his life. This derives from the brain seeing the feelings the person receives from his affair partner as a "survival need" when in truth, he will survive just fine without her. Especially evident when he consider that he once felt that way about his current spouse, which is why he married her.

At its heart, *eros* or passion is a selfish love. It is having a need and seeking to fulfill it. But the other side of the coin is if we don't care, perceive something as not a need, we neglect that object and leave it to rot. Without this love, rebuilding will be much harder simply because we are not motivated to do the hard work of rebuilding. We don't perceive it as a need. Meanwhile, the unfaithful spouse still feels that passion for the affair partner. He has an *eros* love for the affair partner, but a different kind of love for the spouse.

Eros love, then, is a desire and need based love. It is motivated for what we will get out of it. Ideally, in conjunction with the other loves, we are also giving to someone else what they need for their passion. When that happens, you have what is generally termed as "romantic love" in our day. This gives us some insight into how this love works both in marriages and in affairs.

Romantic passion usually starts up in a relationship automatically. That is, most people feel that it happens naturally, without any effort on either person's part. Often it is described as a chemistry between two people. Or the most common term, "falling in love." For true marital love, this love acts as the priming of the marital love pump.

We usually refer to this experience as infatuation. When romantic love fires off between two people, they are both excited about each other. They both fail to see the failings and negative aspects of each other, or if they do, they make excuses or believe they will change, because this powerful love they feel will conquer all, or so it seems.

It should be noted this is the same type of love that one feels during an affair. It produces the "fog" we spoke of in Part 1. The feeling of new love is so powerful that it tends to put blinders on a person so that he cannot see the negative aspects of what he is doing. He only know one thing: "I can't live without having this feeling of love in my life. I must have it." Like a drug addict who is willing to spend their life's savings on the next high, those in affairs don't consider the negative consequences of what they are putting at risk in an affair.

But whether we are talking about a relationship that ends in marriage or one that ends in an affair, eventually this love dies if left unattended. This especially is true with a marriage because of the many distractions. Jobs, bills, children, sports, hobbies, school and many other responsibilities of married couples work to kill off romantic love. Passion dies off like a fire running out of fuel. But even for an affair relationship, eventually it gets old, is not new, the excitement dies off and the two at some point start to feel a responsibility to each other, not to mention the constant worry that they will be discovered and it all come to a sudden end.

This dynamic, the excitement of a new relationship, has led some to conclude that we were not made or created to be monogamous. Most who posit an evolutionary creation of man, point to this as the basic instinct of man that allowed him, especially when man was a small number, to spread his seed as widely as possible for the survival of the species.

However, this fails to account for the totality of love. It places *eros*, passion, romantic love as the only real love, at least as it relates to marriage and creating a family. As we will see, this is an incomplete picture of love. It is only one part, important as it may be. A part that can easily be perverted toward destructive actions in the name of love just as much as the drug addict is willing to steal and kill in the name of his love for the drug.

Because this love is based on an emotional needs-based feeling of well-being, it will naturally go up and down over a period of time. The "honeymoon" eventually dies off. So if we need this type of love in a marriage, how do we keep those fires burning?

This is where the book, *His Needs, Her Needs: How to Affair-proof Your Marriage* by Willard F. Jr. Harley, comes into the picture. This topic is way too big for one article, so I would highly suggest this book be obtained and read for a full understanding, but here is a summary that applies to what we are discussing here.

Men and women tend to have different needs to feel love for someone. One person may perceive a hug as saying, "I love you." Another may feel that when the other does some type of act of service like washing the dishes for them. Another when the person joins them in an activity like a sport or a hobby. While men and women tend to have opposite needs, each person is different. What makes one woman feel loved is not the same for another woman, or one man to another.

Doing the actions that say "I love you" to someone causes them to feel love, and fills what Mr. Harley calls the "love bank." As long as the deposits exceed the withdrawals—doing something that doesn't make them feel loved—the romantic fires are kept going.

The reason that it feels natural in the beginning of a relationship is because each person has an excitement about the relationship that causes them to invest as much time as possible with the other person. When that happens, it makes the other person feel loved. You are each motivated to do for the other the things they want to do. You find yourself spending every spare minute with them.

When I dated Lenita, we were together every evening unless otherwise prevented. When we were together, we focused on each other. I'm sure if I added up the time we spent together, it amounted to at least four to five hours a day on the average. That means we were together, focused on each other, for around 28 hours a week.

But what happened to us? Like all marriages, jobs and children pulled us apart. Over the years, our time spent with each other shrank to minutes a day instead of hours. Often those minutes weren't focused on each other, but on daily issues, taking care of this or that, or attending church. We rarely took time to make deposits into each other's love banks. We had some of the other loves we'll be talking about, so we felt we loved each other, but this love became neglected over the years. It would get fed only on special occasions like Valentine's Day or our anniversary. But nothing like we did during our dating time.

The key then is spending quality time together. Not focused on responsibilities, the children, or a job, but upon each other. Only by spending enough time together can either of you hope to make deposits into the love bank "naturally." Filling those needs comes through quantity of contact. Mr. Harely recommends spending at least 15 hours a week together. That can seem like a lot, but it is an issue of priorities. If one's marriage is important, one will make the time just as easily as you make the time to watch a football game or meet with the guys or any other number of hobbies we may have.

Since discovery day and reading *His Needs, Her Needs*, we've gone from spending a total of one or two hours a week focused on each other to over 15. The result? Despite the affairs, I've never felt more in love with my wife. Even more so than when we were first married.

What occurs naturally at the beginning of a relationship is spending time with each other long enough that we naturally do the actions that say to the other, "I love you." Words are good, but those actions make it real. But as the relationship moves forward, the time together naturally goes down unless the couple makes a conscious effort to counteract it. This requires more than having a night out once a week, though that is a good start. But to make a difference will require spending 15 hours together at least. Find activities you can participate together in.

For instance, here is our usual weekly schedule. Most nights find us swimming at the local gym for around one and a half hours on average including drive time. That amounts to a weekly total of 7.5

hours. Weekly we spend our time on Saturdays going to church together. The car ride is 45 minutes each way, for a total 1.5 hours. Usually she reads a book on marriage enrichment or initially about affairs and dealing with them. That ups the total to 9 hours. We have a weekly eating out together, which invests another 1.5 or more hours a week, bringing it to 10.5 hours a week. Every week, I help her with a cleaning job at an office 30 minutes away. Another hour of drive time alone together, making it 11.5. She usually calls me on her lunch breaks and when she's traveling between jobs, and we talk. This is harder to estimate, but that amounts to at least one hour a day. Add five hours to the total and we spend at least 16.5 hours a week together, focused on each other.

We could add in more smaller pieces, like our texts back and forth, our time in the room when we share things we've found on the computer or discussing some of the issues we've run across on the support forum, but you get the picture. Whereas before the affair we were lucky to spend five minutes focused on each other a day, now it is back to hours. Invest that much time into a relationship, and it becomes hard to not feel loved by them because you are both saying to each other, "You're worth investing my time to be with." Not doing that can't but help to say the opposite.

But that shows how *eros* love works in an affair and why some people become so addicted to that new-relationship excitement, not knowing how to keep it alive, they end up going from one person to another each time the relationship seems to lose its spark and excitement. They don't realize that if they would simply invest the same amount of time with their spouse as they want to do "naturally" with the affair partner, that they would soon feel the same exciting romantic love for them as they do their affair partner.

Romantic, passionate love will rise and fall through a marriage, but if a couple doesn't learn to preserve the time for each other in the face of the other demands, it will fall and rarely rise up. What was natural, spending loads of time with them, now has to be done intentionally. Or more appropriately, the couple needs to intentionally preserve that space and not let other, less important responsibilities, overgrow the love in a marriage. Like weeds need to be pulled from a garden to keep the plants healthy, the marriage has to be tended after planting the seeds through infatuation. Failing to do this is saying the marital garden is not worth saving or preserving.

The danger for the unfaithful spouse, on the other hand, is failing to realize the love they often feel for their affair partner is mostly, if not all, passion, but not the fullness of what love is. The infatuation is the starting gun to trigger a more fuller love, which we will discuss in the next sections. But too many, when they experience this exciting new-relationship romance, mistake it for what love is. By itself, it is a fickle and emotional response to having one's love-needs met by someone else. It is the instinctive response to those triggers that gets romanticized in popular culture as to what love is.

Phileo

The keyword to describe *phileo* love is **friendship**. Most people understand this one well enough. It contains elements of the other loves in a unique combination. Like *eros*, it deepens and is enriched only when we spend time on it. Another more descriptive word, however, is **companionship**. Unlike *eros*, it isn't totally need based, can involve sacrifice, and isn't sexually oriented.

It is when one combines *phileo* love with romantic love that one hits a version of marital love. Yet, even this is not the fullness of marital love. It requires more ingredients. Yet, a marriage that lacks a sense of companionship is a weak marriage indeed.

One of Lenita's songs she always said was our song was "You're My Best Friend" by Queen. We've always had a sense of that friendship, and the subsequent love. But we allowed the companionship to die. We still felt we were friends, we still felt we loved each other, but we had allowed our zest in our relationship to shrivel. It was that lack that her second local affair partner filled, as he talked with her and spent time with her while I was involved in my own world, oblivious to it all.

This thin line between friendship and romantic love is the premise behind the most popular book on the topic of infidelity, *Not Just Friends* by Shirley Glass. Friendship can entail intimacy to a degree, and intense love for the other person, only minus the more sexual overtones and romantic love. If two people who become close friends find they are becoming romantically attracted to each other, it becomes very easy to justify to one's self that "we're just friends." As Lenita thought at the time, "I can handle this and not let it evolve into an affair," all the while she was already neck deep into the affair. Blurring the lines between friendship and romantic love is the fertile grounds for affairs to blossom.

How does one identify if a friendship is moving into romantic love? One can identify it by answering the following questions. Do either of you flirt with the other? Do you spend more time talking and interacting with the friend than your own spouse? When you talk, do you regularly discuss intimate details like marital problems you are dealing with, or sexual preferences? Do you make contact via text, phone, or email/messages multiple times every day? Do you think about them daily? Do you sense an attraction to them, or what many people would call "chemistry"?

If you can answer yes to any of these questions, it should serve as a warning flag that this relationship has the potential to be more than just friends, and you should take steps to establish firm boundaries and prevent alone time. Limit contact and use techniques to guard your thoughts so as to not allow the spark to start a fire.

If you answered yes to several of these questions, you are likely already involved in the early stages of an affair, whether you've even kissed or held hands yet. Pulling back and dialing down the contact to once or twice a week is the only way to preserve the friendship and avoid damaging your marriage.

True friendship is a great blessing. Each person in the marriage can benefit from having friends outside the marriage. As John Gray says in *Why Mars and Venus Collide*, it is important that each spouse find other sources of friendship outside the marriage so that the spouse isn't left to provide all of one's well-being. Women need other women to talk to, and men need other males to interact with. Our society has more and more limited friendships, especially among men.

When dealing with friendships of the opposite sex or any person one may be attracted to, boundaries are important. It is usually the ignoring of those boundaries that leads to a friendship evolving into a romantic relationship. Avoid spending alone time with such an individual. Always have someone else with you. Avoid discussing marital issues or other intimate details reserved for a marital relationship or professional therapist. If he wants to text or contact you frequently, send signals you're not available all the time, like waiting for a few hours to answer a text, or a quick text back that you are involved in something and can't chat now. Enough of those and he'll get the signal in most cases.

When you see several of these warning signs growing, that is the time to run. Don't think you can handle it. You're already hooked if these things are happening. The deeper in you go from there, the harder it will be to stop the affair and the more danger to your marriage as the addictive nature of what you are feeling takes over.

Perhaps you have heard some unfaithful spouses say they just wanted the sex, not a relationship. In effect, they wanted the *eros* love without the *phileo*. They want the pleasure of sex without the entanglements of a relationship. They are in love with the feelings, not the person. Therefore, they don't care from whom they get them, just so they get them. Is this possible?

In short, yes, to a degree. It is possible for someone to want only the sex and not love the person involved or desire a friendship with them. That was the attitude of Clyde, Lenita's first affair partner. He didn't want to know about her, her family, or any details of her life and history. He just wanted sexual favors, period. In effect, he didn't want to be one with her emotionally. This is the basis of prostitution. A man can pay for it, and not have any strings attached. He may never see that girl again.

However, to say this creates no emotional or marital bonds is a secular view of sex as a form of recreation and not much more. Only when it is linked with love for the person does it take on any meaning whatsoever in a bonding fashion, per that view. As we will see in the next chapter, this is an incomplete picture of sex. Rather, sexual intercourse involves making the two into one flesh. Whoever one has sex with, joins with them in the basic act of matrimony. A bond is created, no matter how much love is or is not felt for the person. In other words, yes one can avoid *phileo* love with another individual, but *eros* love has its own bonding with the other that cannot be escaped.

Storge

The two words that describe this type of love is **comforting affection**. Its use in Greek is mostly restricted to family relationships, but can expand into a more broader "family" among friends.

In the popular TV show of the 80s, "Star Trek, the Next Generation," one of the characters was named Data, a sentient android. In seeking to define a friend or even romantic relationship, he described it as, "My neurological pathways have become accustom to your presence." This is the essentially the definition of *storge* love, but in a more biological sense. We become accustom to those around us, extended family and friends, and develop an affection for them that we find comforting. We enjoy being with them because we find security in their presence. It also tends to include biological connections, though not exclusively.

Often when a hurt spouse learns about the affair, he will bounce between hate and love for his unfaithful spouse. He is angry that the spouse chose someone over or in addition to him, equating to a rejection of his love. This negatively affects his romantic and companionship love. Yet, he is accustom to the unfaithful spouse's presence and doesn't want to lose the security of that relationship, especially if they have been together for years.

This love also interacts in concern for the children. Not wanting a broken family, some stay together for the sake of the children. *Storge* love is involved in such decisions. The hurt spouse doesn't want to deny the children the relationship with their father or mother, so for the sake of the children and keeping the family whole, they stay together even if the love between them is dead or dying.

The unfaithful spouse experiences this love when he feels he loves his spouse and doesn't want to divorce, but he no longer feels "in love" with the hurt spouse. What he means is he no longer feels any *eros* love, especially when compared to the excitement of the affair partner, but he still feels the bonds of *storge* love with his spouse, the mother or father of their children. That relationship is familiar, comfortable, and provides security. There is a history to that relationship, unlike with the affair partner.

In a healthy marriage, this love grows with time spent together. As the years pass, each grows accustom to the other's presence. With the advent of biological children, this bond grows exponentially. A family is created, and the love for one's child extends to the spouse who is also a parent and who contributed their DNA to create this child bonding the two into one, literal flesh.

To the degree Lenita and I felt true love for each other before the affair started, this and the next love, for me, defined why we felt we loved each other. We didn't take into account, as important as this love was, that it was not the totality of what marital love should be. After 29 years and three children, our *storge* love was very strong. But our *phileo, eros*, and in Lenita's case to a degree, *agape* love had waned.

Agape

Agape is also one of the loves little understood. Most think of it in terms of divine love, or non-sexual love as contrasted with *eros*. But these ideas only skirt the foundation of the word and its corresponding love.

If there is one word I would list to describe what this type of love involves, it would be **martyr**. Unlike *eros*, it is not based on filling one's needs. Unlike *phileo*, it doesn't require companionship. Contrasted with *storge*, it is not based on family bonds or a comforting presence. Rather, this love indicates one who is willing to sacrifice themselves for another, a cause, or a belief.

In classic Greek, the term was rarely used, and was a more generic word for love without a lot of meaning attached to it. The writers of the New Testament infused the word with the meaning of love that God has for us. But there are three times in the Bible when the word is not used of divine love, but inappropriate love. It is the highest form of love one can have. It willingly sacrifices what one wants in favor of the needs and desires of the one loved. This is why Jesus said, "Greater love hath no man than this, that a man lay down his life for his friends." (Joh 15:13 ASV)

The term became attached to divine love because God's love so often uses the term. Because Israel so often committed adultery against Him, and He forgave them and took them back. Because we so often seek other "gods" in our lives than Him, and yet He waits with open arms to receive us again like the father did the prodigal son. For sure, the pure example of *agape* love is God Himself, who willingly became incarnate as a man, so He could give His life, to defeat death, and restore life through His resurrection. In spite of the fact that we, as a whole, had rejected Him.

None of us can hope to have and exhibit a pure *agape* love, but we can participate in it through Him. Our love involves selfish desires, need-based companionship. We can't get away from that, and indeed, should not. For us, *agape* love transforms those loves into an integrated whole of what love should be.

St. Paul exhorts the Ephesians in relation to marriage: "Husbands, love your wives, even as Christ also loved the church, and gave himself up for it;" (Eph 5:25 ASV) Marriage is at its ideal, a sacrifice of each other on the altar of their new spouse. In the Orthodox Church's marriage ceremony, this is illustrated with crowns the groom and bride wear on their heads, known as crowns of martyrdom. This same spirit is shown in the traditional Western marriage vows, "...for better or for worse."

This type of love does not waver with one's feelings of love. It does not rely upon being treated fairly or justly by the other spouse.

It does not even depend upon whether one's spouse is abusive or not. Once one has *agape* love for another, it is there forever.

Note, I'm not saying this love puts up with abuse or injustice anymore than God puts up with sin. Simply that one loves the other, and has their best interest at heart no matter what happens or what sacrifices need to be made.

Allow me to illustrate this with my own situation, at the risk of sounding puffed up and wanting praise from my readers. For I don't count this as something I did through great effort, but was simply there and natural, so I attribute it to God working in me when I needed it most.

When I first discovered Lenita's affairs, among the shock, denial, and disbelief that I would ever find myself in this situation, one desire rose above the others. I realized she had committed a mortal sin that could destroy our marriage and her. While not denying my pain and struggle, my first concern was for redeeming her if at all possible.

So much so that when I called my priest the next morning, he asked me whether I wanted a divorce or not. I said without hesitation, as if there could be any doubt so why ask, that I did not want a divorce. The idea of divorcing her hadn't even entered my mind, though I worried that it could end there depending on where she was at. I readily forgave her, and that has stuck. I've never dangled her sin over her head as a punishment.

That said, *agape* love would have demanded that I leave if she continued to reject me. If she had not repented within a reasonable amount of time, like the sinner cannot be with God in heaven, I would have had to leave her. That in itself would have been a sacrifice on my part because I wouldn't want to do that. Yet, if she stood any chance of healing, it would require at some point for me to release her like the father did the prodigal son. But no matter what, I would still love her, no matter what she did. For that, my pain would be all the more deep. But it is far less than the pain God has for the many who have rejected Him, and He still so loved the world that He sent His only-begotten son to rescue us through the sacrifice of death.

It is *agape* love that ties the other loves together into a full, complete, and holy love that goes beyond ourselves. You cannot "fall out of love" with *agape* love. The heart of a marital love is this self-sacrificial love.

Allow me to put it in the negative. Many look at love as merely a feeling, an emotional attachment. It is that, but by itself, it falls far short. So when during the marriage, the one spouse isn't getting the sexual love he wants or expects, instead of being willing to sacrifice for a time, he goes outside the marriage to find his fulfillment. When one spouse neglects the other, and someone comes along who pays attention to him, he mistakes that attention for true love because he doesn't have a sacrificial love for his spouse that no matter the temptation presented, he will abstain. *Agape* love does not ebb and flow with circumstances, but with one's commitment to be a martyr for the benefit of the other person.

I know what some are thinking. Doormat. No, not quite, as I illustrated above. *Agape* love doesn't shield the object of love from the consequences of his actions, but loves him, even when that love says you must release him in the hope that he will eventually repent and return with a true change of heart. That is often harder than staying and shielding him from the consequences of his actions, and ends up enabling his sin instead of healing it.

What is True Marital Love?

All love contains elements of each flavor of love. It is not like you can take love and neatly divide it into these black and white categories. *Storge* love for a child involves a level of *eros* passion for him. The parents sacrifice often for the well-being and benefit of the child, exhibiting true *agape* love. All human *agape* love is connected to *eros, phileo*, and *storge* love.

In each action, one type of love tends to dominate over the others in time, while for a full love, all comes under the umbrella of *agape* love in general. For if love doesn't mean to give of one's self for the betterment of the other, then in what manner is it true love? In what manner is instinctive and needs-based love really love in the full sense of the word if it does not have as its final goal the best for the other person, even at your expense?

The ironic aspect of a full love of this nature is that one gets more than what the other loves can give by themselves. Our fulfillment doesn't come from getting, but in giving. It is the nature of this type of love to establish love as a lasting love.

While in my story I've attributed several aspects of what Lenita did to rebuilding as key in my quick recovery, if there is one reason why I healed as fast as I did, much quicker than most people in my support group, is that this sacrificial love caused me to be more concerned for her than for myself. I was more focused on her healing than my own. I forgave her readily, even though I didn't know if her commitment would stick. As I write this, not even two years past discovery day, I don't think about the affairs much. It is always there, but I don't hurt as much from it. I don't get depressed over it anymore. Our relationship is better than it has ever been. I'm exceedingly thankful that she was able to repent and turn from the path she was headed down. It has been a long and painful process, but a rewarding one for both of us.

To put it bluntly, without a strong sense of love embracing all the loves, especially agape love, I would still be hurting today. I would feel the injustice of what she did to me, the grief of what I had lost would still weigh heavily on my heart. Despite the fact she'd done all the right things so that other hurt spouses on the support group vocally wish their spouses were like her, I would still hurt deep inside, not feeling free to relinquish my pain for fear it would let her off the hook. I would not have easily forgiven her. If it were not for a love that didn't depend upon her behavior to exist, I would not have sacrificed my own selfish desires for what was best for both of us. Instead of enjoying a fulfilling relationship with her now, we would live in doubt and stress, fearing the next slip up and that love would shatter with the next sin.

If passion love, family affection love, and companionship love do not lead one to sacrificial love, then that love is a shadow of the real thing, and not fully love. If love can so readily changed based upon feelings and actions of others, then it is not true love, but selfish ego-protecting desires.

As St. Paul states: "Love is patient, love is kind; love does not envy; love does not boast, is not puffed up; does not behave disgracefully, does not seek its own, is not provoked to anger, thinks no evil; does not rejoice over unrighteousness, but rejoices with the truth; bears all things, believes all things, hopes all things, endures all things."(1Co 13:4-7 EMTV)

Are you in love? Let that love be the mark by which you measure if you are there. If we are honest, none of us exhibit it perfectly. But we strive to do so, and if we don't, only then have we lost.

Marriage and Sex

One of the conclusions I've come to in going through the whole infidelity issue is a stronger sense of both what marriage is and how our society's cultural values tend to undermine it.

In this day and age, many who have yet to marry think there is nothing wrong with having sex with whoever you wish. Even among many Christians, while nodding in agreement that fornication is bad, will consider teens having sex as inevitable. Who remains a virgin until they're married anymore? Premarital sex is a given. Some even consider it a time to "sow their wild oats" and get it out of their system before getting married.

Is it no wonder why so many get married and then find that attitude hard to shut off simply because they made a commitment? Especially if that activity before marriage became a hard-to-break habit or if hard times hit the marriage and that "for better or worse" commitment feels too confining. Add in the cultural messages that guys can cheat as long as they don't get caught, growing up in cheating households so it seems to be the normal marital relationship, and the justification of what marriage is and what sex is about, and you have a recipe for many broken homes and marriages.

The big disconnect that I see is the lack of understanding the relationship between marriage and sex. Sex in our society is generally understood as first an enjoyable activity that ideally you do with someone you love. Much like going to see a movie is fun, but even better to go see it with someone you enjoy spending time with.

But there is a big, big difference. Going to see a movie doesn't produce children and create a family. My understanding after having studied this for years, and now within the context of infidelity, is that sex does what it has historically always done: consummate a marriage. It can never be done in isolation from that bond it creates. Which means that every sex act a teen or pre-legal-marriage couple have is the consummation of a marriage. Any subsequent sex acts with another is adultery.

This is made clear when Jesus talked about adultery:

> They said, "Moses permitted a man to write a certificate of divorce, and to put her away." And Jesus answered and said to them, "In view of your hardheartedness he wrote this commandment for you. But from the beginning of the creation, God 'made them male and female. For this reason a man shall leave his father and mother and be joined to his wife, and the two shall become one flesh'; so then they are no longer two, but one flesh. Therefore what God has united together, let not man separate." (Mar 10:4-9 EMTV)

The "two shall become one flesh" is frequently cited as relating to marriage in Genesis and by Jesus here. This details the essence of what marriage is about. But what does it mean? The Jewish understanding has been that Adam and Eve both came from one body, and marriage was designed to unite them back into one body. But obviously this does not happen literally. Or does it?

Yes, it does, in the child produced from the act of sexual union. A child contains the DNA of both husband and wife, and can be literally said to be the two becoming one. Having a child doesn't make one married, but by participating in the act of life-creating sexual intercourse. By the couple doing the activity which can and does bring forth oneness of the two flesh in a new life, whether or not it is ever realized in an actual child, bonds the two individuals as one. Both for the purpose of uniting back to oneness in life and companionship ("It is not good for man to be alone."), but also in the procreation of the literal fulfillment of the two becoming one flesh through a child by creating a nurturing family unit.

You'll note that the act of sex, which brings about the oneness of the two individuals, is followed by Jesus' statement, "What God has united together, let not man separate." Once that bond has been formed, it should not be broken, for God now considers the couple "married." Any act of sex with another person, though not legally or socially a marriage, forms a marital bond by becoming one flesh with that person. Such is not the fullness of marriage by any means, which makes the physical marriage all the more of a violation for it becomes a joke. The meaning and reality of what is being done degrades the value of sex as a bonding in marriage to another, especially when it is broken repeatedly, multiple times, all to have a "fun time." It means nothing more than going to see a movie with a good friend does.

To see this, it is helpful to know how marriage ceremonies were done in biblical times. Over the years, it varied in one point or another, but the following principles are consistent. First came the betrothal. This isn't like our current engagement, but a legal contract for the two parties to be married. For all legal purposes, once the betrothal was signed by the parents and witnessed (not by a state...that came much later in history), the couple were considered married and any sex with another was considered adultery. If either party wanted to not go through with it, they had to get a divorce, even before the wedding ceremony. This was the contractual part of the marriage. They were pledged to each other, and to break the contract had consequences. But marriage was not complete until the wedding, which could be as short as a few months to as long as a year in most cases.

At the wedding, there are prayers prayed over wine. The ceremonies varied here and became more formalized as it became expected that rabbis would officiate. In Jesus' day, it was not a given as it was not prescribed by the Jewish law that a rabbi had to be there. But at one point, the couple would retire to a special room to consummate the marriage. A cloth would be thrown out showing her blood, indicating she was a virgin. At this point, the marriage was fulfilled, and the wedding would continue for several days with a lot of partying.

The act of the couple going into a private room to consummate the marriage with sexual intercourse is still done in modern Jewish wedding ceremonies, though symbolically:

> "After the ceremony ends, the bride and groom retire to a private room, called Heder Yichud, to symbolically 'consummate' the marriage. In the room, the couple breaks their fast and takes a few moments to relax together before going to greet all the wedding guests at the party." (http://judaism.about.com/od/weddings/ss/wedding_how_9.htm)

Point being, there are several ways that a couple becomes one. Legally, emotionally, socially, spiritually, and physically. It is expected that by the time one physically unites as one, that the others will be in place so that the act is fulfilling a reality and not a sham. But let's reverse this. If you have all the other unions save the physical one, what do you have? You have two people who are in love, that is, a very strong friendship (it is hoped) of the most intimate and strong kind, who have maybe committed themselves to certain legal agreements, sharing of lives and living, etc., but without becoming one flesh. A relationship without the possibility of generating life from the union of the two to potentially create one flesh.

What you are left with is a very strong friendship with some legal commitments, but you do not have what God understands as marriage, that is, the two becoming one flesh. Consummating the marriage with sex ties all the commitments and pledges together, and seals the union by participating together in the potential creation of one flesh. Without it, the concept of marriage falls apart, and there isn't a real marital union. With it, you have a real marriage and union of two people.

Therefore, to have sex with another is to consummate a marriage with them. While the concept of "not falling in love with someone, but just having sex with them" is true, as some unfaithful spouses say, the reason that sexual intercourse with someone other than one's spouse is considered adultery is because you have literally married another person. It may not be emotional for the person(s) involved, but it should be, because they are eternally united themselves before God as one flesh. Whether a person feels any love in that or not is irrelevant to what they are actually doing. Not loving the affair partner is better as far as dealing with the rebuilding, but it divorces one's spouse and marries another all the same.

Because our society, even among Christians, has lost this understanding of what sex is about in relation to marriage, we have not only high rates of "one flesh" children born outside of a family structure, abortions, and low moral standards as to reserving one's self for one's future spouse, but we also have such a high rate of infidelity and adultery once people are legally married to someone.

Because once sex is no longer viewed as a marital bond, all that is left is a commitment made on a piece of paper with the state and vows in a ceremony, but no commitment and value attached to the act of sex itself beyond having a good time. Too many view marriage as nothing more than a legal agreement governed by the state, and/or a socially acceptable way to have sex with someone you feel you care about. Historically, that has not been what marriage was about. Therefore, when the caring is no longer there, when the romance has died, then the point of marriage and sex seem to demand one find it where one can, since the spouse is no longer providing what one felt the purpose of marriage to be.

But a proper view of sex as the sacrament of union within a marriage puts an understanding of what sex is about and how it is often so misused. If this proper understanding prevailed in our culture, adultery, infidelity, and divorce would be much, much lower. As long as it isn't, many people won't so easily be able to flip the switch and see sex as something to reserve for only one person, the one they will marry, and raise a family of two fleshes becoming one without violating that bond.

Marriage, Divorce, and Adultery: A Biblical Study to Dispel Myths

Those having been affected by adultery of a spouse tend to have various views or memories of what Jesus said about the subject and when one is "allowed" to end a marriage.

When the Pharisees approached Jesus to ask him whether it was lawful to put away a woman, Jesus asks them what did the Law say:

> They said, "Moses permitted a man to write a certificate of divorce, and to put her away." And Jesus answered and said to them, "In view of your hardheartedness he wrote this commandment for you. But from the beginning of the creation, God 'made them male and female.' 'For this reason a man shall leave his father and mother and be joined to his wife, and the two shall become one flesh'; so then they are no longer two, but one flesh. Therefore what God has united together, let not man separate." (Mar 10:4-9 EMTV)

This tells us several things about marriage as it relates to adultery and divorce. First, that it is God's ideal that this union between a man and woman be permanent. Anything short of that is sin. But we now need to define what sin is so that we understand what follows.

Sin is any deviation from the ideal that God designed us for. Thus the phrase, "falling short of the glory of God." Actions are sinful because they are destructive to ourselves, our relationship to God, and our relationship to others. The antithesis of the Great Commandment, to love the Lord your God with all your heart, soul, mind, and body, and your neighbor as yourself. So we are not talking about some arbitrary set of rules that God one day sat down and said to himself, "Hum, what do they enjoy doing that I don't want them to do, because I'm just a kill-joy?" They are sins because they destroy us.

Think of it like this. When Ford builds a car, they design it to be used effectively under certain parameters. So it makes a great tool for getting from one place to another. It makes a lousy can opener. It just isn't designed for it. While someone might find a sharp spot on the car where he can open a can of beans, he's much more likely to cut himself than if he pulled out a can opener.

So what Jesus is saying here is that this is how God designed marriage to work. Divorce wasn't the original plan behind it. So anytime divorce is present, it is a falling short somewhere, and sin is involved.

But Jesus goes on to explain why this is so. The fact that He made a male and a female, and they can be joined together so that no longer are they two fleshes, but one, is the definition of marriage as I laid out in the previous chapter. By using "flesh," He is emphasizing that this is not just some metaphysical, abstract spiritual unity, though it is that. It is not just an emotional bonding, though it is that. It is a physical bonding. That is unique to marriage. We can have good friends that we dearly love, have a deep spiritual bond with, and feel like soul sisters or brothers, but we are not married to them. Because there is no sexual relationship.

So it is the sexual act itself that brings about the one-fleshness of the two people. This has other implications, but for the matter of adultery, it describes why committing a sexual act with someone is in essence bonding yourself to them in marriage. Consequently, any sexual union to another is committing the sin of adultery by divorcing your spouse and physically "remarrying" another. Jesus goes on to say:

> "Whoever should put away his wife and marry another commits adultery against her. And if a wife should put away her husband and be married to another, she commits adultery." (Mar 10:11-12 EMTV)

Why is this so? Because the man and woman have already been joined to one another. So if one puts the other away, and marries another, he or she is bonding themselves to another while still bonded to the first, thus breaking asunder the first bond. Having sex with another, in effect, violates that first bonding. You are becoming "one flesh" with a new person, and therefore breaks asunder what God has joined with the spouse. This is destructive to all involved, that is, sinful.

"So, is everyone headed to Hell, then, who divorces and marries another?" Not necessarily. Yes, it is sin. That is, it is a corrupted form of what God designed. But as Jesus notes, Moses gave them the law that they could put away their spouse because we live in a sinful world, and sometimes, due to the hardness of the hearts of one or both spouses, it doesn't work out. While it is a corruption, when one person is intent on having it their way, there is little that can be done. Practical realities of living in a fallen world have to be considered.

Sometimes, despite the best efforts by one spouse, divorce is the only option left and to remain unmarried would lead to worse sins. So sometimes the sin, while not the ideal, is the "least of all evils." Forgiveness and healing of the broken relationship and marital bond has to happen, but may be preferable to living, for example, in an abusive situation that could have life-long negative effects upon the spouse and/or the children. But those realities don't detract from the truth of the matter, that due to our sinful hearts, we sometimes end up having to resort to divorce, and the result of that is unless both spouses keep themselves pure, one or both parties can end up committing adultery.

Some people use these verses to suggest that divorce is only allowed by Jesus under the narrow grounds of adultery or fornication by one's spouse. But that is not what Jesus is saying. All divorce isn't "allowed" if one wants to keep sin free. But what Jesus is saying is that the only time a person doesn't themselves commit the sin of adultery in divorcing a spouse to remarry is when their spouse has already committed adultery. In that narrow instance, the divorcing spouse isn't committing adultery, they are responding to adultery already committed. The bonds have already in essence been violated and broken. Divorce at that point is only admitting and recognizing that sin, not committing it.

Also there is no command from God that if one spouse commits adultery, that the other has to divorce them, as some erroneously interpret these verses. Nor does it mean it is the only time the Scriptures say you can divorce a spouse. It only means it is the only time you can do so and not commit adultery yourself. But in any divorce and remarriage, one or both of the spouses is, will, or has committed adultery.

So, if the physical act of sex can form and break the bonds of "one flesh," then where does emotional affairs come into play? First, let's define what we mean by emotional affairs. Emotional affairs are when we become intimate with another person when that intimacy should be reserved for one's spouse. Note, we're talking about affairs here, not adultery. More on that in a minute. But the marriage is about more than physical intimacy, but also emotional and spiritual. The sexual bond adds an extra dimension of intimacy to the emotional and spiritual bonds that takes them beyond normal friendship.

So, when a spouse spends more time emotionally bonding with someone of the opposite sex than he does his spouse, that is, as Shirley Glass in *Not Just Friends* says, closing a window on your spouse and opening one to someone else. When you discuss marital problems and sexual issues with such a person, you are sharing things that should remain between you and your spouse, or at most, a counselor, therapist, or doctor. When one sex chats with others online, he is sharing a part of their intimate sexual life with others, even if he never see them or will ever have physical contact with them. It is something that should only be shared with one's spouse.

When does an emotional affair become adulterous? Jesus lays it out quite plainly:

> "You have heard that it was said, 'You shall not commit adultery.' But I say to you, that whoever looks at a woman in order to lust after her has already committed adultery with her in his heart. (Mat 5:27-28 EMTV)

This needs to be explained a bit, because too many think if a man or woman looks at another appreciatively or even what many men will experience, "admiring the view," that it is lusting. But the word "lust" means literally a very strong desire. We're not talking a little desire here. We're talking, "If I could find a way to get her in bed, I'd do it in a heartbeat" desire. You're not just drawn to the attractiveness of a woman or man, you are "lusting after" him or her, craving them, wanting to have sex with them, whether you ever do or not. Jesus is saying, when you have that kind of desire for the woman, you've already committed adultery. Because if you could, you would.

So an emotional affair, if it leads one to seriously desire another person sexually, whether or not it is practical to go after them or not, has turned as adulterous as if you'd hopped in bed with them right then. So yes, someone who is sex chatting on line, with no desire or intention of ever meeting up with the people they are chatting with nor any desire to want sex with them, hasn't committed adultery yet, but that doesn't mean they aren't having an affair. An affair covers any inappropriate relationship that moves into the areas of intimacy reserved for one's spouse. Not just physically having sex with someone, or even desiring to. Having an affair is broader than committing adultery. A person can have an affair without committing adultery.

Finally, all this talk about the sin of adultery and how easily we can end up committing it, even when we really don't want to, it is important to remember that God does forgive, especially when it is near impossible for us to avoid running into it due to the hardness of a heart. Many will recall the story of the woman caught in adultery. The rulers brought her to Jesus to test him, saying that she should be stoned according to the law of Moses, because she was caught red-handed in the act. Then Jesus told them, "He who is without sin, cast the first stone." Then they all walked away. Then Jesus saw that her accusers had walked away, He said, "Woman, where are those accusers of yours? Has no one condemned you?" When she said no one, He said, "Neither do I condemn you; go, and from now on sin no more." (John 8:3-11 EMTV)

Did you catch what Jesus did here? Yeah, he beat the Pharisees at their own game, once again. Instead of tripping up Jesus, they all walked away in shame because they knew they were not without sin themselves. But that's not what I'm talking about. Think about it. Sitting before this woman caught in the act of adultery was the very God who had given the law that she should be stoned. Of all the people there that day, He was the only one without sin. He was the only one who could have cast the first stone. But He refused to do so. He refused to condemn her by picking up a stone Himself. He could have, and would have been justified to do so. But He had compassion on her instead and knew she could be more than a harlot, an adulteress, a sinner. She could be redeemed. Church tradition says that she did end up a saint in the Church.

So whether you end up committing adultery by divorcing and remarrying, whether unavoidable or not, or because of bad decisions that led you down that path of succumbing to temptation, there is healing and forgiveness. There is life instead of death, if we are willing to allow God to turn our lives around, and heal us so that we become committed to go and sin no more.

Conclusion

There are no guarantees in life. There are certainly no guarantees in infidelity and rebuilding. Even in marriage. Our fallen condition and fallen world will see to that. Anyone who thinks they and their spouse are immune to infidelity are living in delusion. It is that delusion that leaves a couple vulnerable to affairs.

I've seen victims of infidelity lament losing the innocent trust they held in their spouse. Problem is, such trust is blind. It is natural to think, "It can't happen to me," until of course it does. Even though I knew it wasn't impossible, I didn't think it would ever happen to me. It did.

Oh yes. There is the expectation of faithfulness in marriage. As Jesus said, faithfulness is in the design specs of a healthy marriage. But to build a house on the Gulf coast and not build it to withstand a hurricane is taking an unnecessary risk. Few build expecting a hurricane to hit, but they know it is possible and so prepare.

So there is the expectation of faithfulness, but nurturing the marriage through the years to avoid the hurricane of infidelity and provide healing if one hits is still necessary because we are a fallen people living in a fallen world. Trust that ignores these realities is trust waiting to be destroyed. The only one who should engender that kind of trust from us is God Himself.

In rebuilding, likewise, there are no guarantees. We have given you a snapshot of our marriage and how Lenita was lead into a series of affairs that violated her morals and personal beliefs. We've also painted a picture of how we rebuilt from that. We've made significant strides in recovery over the past 21 months. There have been some setbacks, but relatively few compared to most people. We've attempted to give you a picture of what a successful rebuilding looks like.

Today as I write this, an event occurred yesterday that illustrates perfectly the lack of a guarantee of success. Yesterday, February 20, 2013, marked 21 months and 9 days since discovery day for me. Yesterday, Bubba made a surprise call to Lenita. It has been around 18 months since he'd made any significant attempt to contact her, and even longer since she'd actually responded to any of his attempts. The last instance was in June 2011 when he placed a note on her car and she placed one on his.

I'd like to say she handled the surprise call well. But she didn't recognize him until he told her who he was. He called on a number she'd not seen before. Caught by surprise, when he asked her if they could talk a minute, she did what came natural to her and said yes. They had a brief but non-inappropriate conversation.

To her credit, her intention in engaging him was to convince him she was doing well and our marriage was strong. His wife had cheated on him, and after 2 years their rebuilding fell apart. So we guessed he hoped ours would be as well since we are near the two year mark ourselves. There were no exchanges of "I miss you" and "I love you" type language. Just "how are you doing?"

Also, once it was over, she immediately told me all about it at the next available opportunity. As she has done since discovery day, she remains transparent, keeping no secrets from me. Doing this convinces me she is being honest. If she wanted contact with him, she would have hid their conversation from me, not confessed it.

Yet she did break no contact. Instead of telling him, "Sorry, I cannot engage you in conversation. Please don't make contact with me again," and hang up, she said, "Yes" and proceeded to communicate with him, effectively breaking no contact. She knew, from all we've studied, talked about, and given advice on, that keeping no contact is critical. Yet when faced with it, she caved to his desire to talk with her.

She was distressed that she allowed this to happen, again. Shortly after discovery day, we could chalk it up to her emotional attachment to Bubba as to why she found it so hard to not respond. Now, when she testifies that she didn't feel anything for him, she still felt obligated to respond. She labeled it a "wake-up call."

The event has revealed a short coming in her character. So she has scheduled counseling for helping her to evaluate why she has a hard time with this issue. She called our priest and discussed it with him. We have both talked about it all day off and on since we were working together. She is determined to fix this issue because she knows the future health of our marriage is on the line.

This setback, when I've felt for some time we'd been doing very well, is a reminder of how easily a marriage ignored can become broken, faltering, and encountering a "warp core breach." It is possible that five or ten years from now, you might hear that we are divorced. At this point, that appears to be an unlikely outcome. But it is a possible outcome if we are both not diligent to avoid boundary crossing and playing with fire.

To that end, like one is always an alcoholic, no matter how long they've been sober, infidelity will now always be part of our history as a couple. To believe we've "arrived," are fully healed, can handle playing in the fire, to believe we are invulnerable, that we say to ourselves, "it will never happen to me," is the point when we are the most susceptible to becoming unfaithful.

There are no guarantees, so we must be ever vigilant to guard the marriage and avoid seeing how close to the edge we can get without falling off.

We pray our story and the articles have given you some tools, some support, some information, and inspiration to find your own path to the healing of infidelity and emerge on the other side in a vibrant marital relationship. Don't stop learning, growing, and enriching your relationship. The results are rewarding.

More Information

For more information and help, visit our website:
http://www.healinginfidelity.com

We also run a discussion forum:
http://forum.healinginfidelity.com

The authors appreciate any feedback and honest reviews at our site and/or at your favorite online retailing establishments.

About the Authors

Rick Copple

Rick grew up in South/Central Texas, and attended college at Southern Nazarene University where he graduated with a BA in religion. He pastored two churches before moving to the Orthodox Church in 1996. During those years and up through the present, he wrote many homilies, Bible studies, and devotionals.

In 2005, Rick became interested in writing science fiction and fantasy stories. He has currently published seven book, six fiction and one non-fiction book not counting this one, under the pen name: R. L. Copple. You can discover more about his fiction writing at his author website: http://www.rlcopple.com.

Rick did most of the initial writing of the book, but Lenita wrote much of the real-life story, as well as was highly involved in the editing of the manuscript. Much of what the two learned about healing infidelity came through her healing.

Lenita Copple

Lenita grew up in Bethany, Oklahoma. After marrying Rick, she spent most of her time raising the kids as a stay-at-home mom. However, she earned extra money doing child care and house cleaning over the years. For a period of time she home-schooled the kids when they were young.

Always devoted to her kids and a partner in her marriage, she felt she hurt herself as well as Rick by giving into the temptation to have an affair, something she never imagined she'd ever do until it happened. But her determination and commitment in rebuilding not only salvaged the marriage, but healed the relationship. Through it, she's re-proved her love to her husband and to God.

Acknowledgments

We offer thanks to all involved in our recovery. From our priest, our therapist, family and friends who rode the early days with us and offered prayers, and especially to all our friends at Daily Strength support forum, whose names we'll probably never know for most of them. Each one has, in their own way, been a part of our rebuilding and had a hand in our journey, which is still continuing.

I'd also like to thank my beta-readers who helped edit the book. Any and all typos, grammar mistakes, and other annoying habits are entirely my own fault. But much thanks goes out for the errors that were caught and corrected to make this as reader-friendly as possible.

Finally, we thank God for His grace and love in helping us to rebuild to a better, more vibrant relationship. May He use this book to aid others to not only save their marriage, but redeem their relationship to a vibrant health.

Made in United States
Orlando, FL
30 January 2023

29232486R00124